Researching Adventures
Challenging GLYPH-Making Activities
in
Language Arts, Math, Science, & Social Studies

by Laura Magner

© 2005 Pieces of Learning
CLC0330
ISBN 1-931334-43-9
www.piecesoflearning.com
Printed in the U.S.A.

All rights reserved. In our effort to produce high quality educational products we offer portions of this book as "reproducible." Permission is granted, therefore, to the buyer - one teacher - to reproduce student activity pages in LIMITED quantities for students in the buyer's classroom only. The right to reproduce is not extended to other teachers, entire schools, or to school systems.
Use of any pages on the Internet is strictly forbidden. No other part of this publication may be reproduced in whole or part. The whole publication may not be stored in a retrieval system, or transmitted in any form or by any means, electronic, mechanical, photocopying, recording, or otherwise without written permission of the publisher.
For any other use contact Pieces of Learning at 1-800-729-5137.
For a complete catalog of products contact Pieces of Learning
or visit our Web Site at www.piecesoflearning.com

Table of Contents

Introduction 5
National Educational Standards 6
    English 6
    Math 7
    Science 8
    Social Studies 9
    Technology 9
Getting Started 11
Teacher Tips 12
Apple GLYPH Early Elementary Example 13
Monster of Nice GLYPH Sample Directions 15

Language Arts GLYPHS 16-30
Cereal Box 17
Octopus 20
Candy 23
"Good Morning" Soda 26
Flag 29

Math GLYPHS 31-43
Mystery Number 32
Wrist Watch 34
Great Dessert 37
Computer 39
Flag II 41

Science GLYPHS 44-52
Collage 45
Fishy Friends 47
Porch Pet 49
Sunshowy 51

Social Studies GLYPHS 53-71
The Monster of Nice 54
Back to School 57
Fan Mail 59
Mama's New Hat 61
Lighthouse Island 63
Make a Map 66
Teddy Bear 69

Appendix 72-79

Introduction

A <u>glyph</u> is an activity that derives its name from *hieroglyphics*. Just as Egyptian hieroglyphics used several symbols to convey one sentence or thought, glyphs use pieces and symbols to create a product. <u>Researching Adventures → Creating Great "GLYPHS"</u> is a more challenging take on the familiar glyph activity. After research, data collection, and organization, the student puts together the pieces to form a finished project.

Why use Great Glyphs?

This collection of glyph activities challenges students to use multiple research techniques. Students need to **read** non-fiction texts, **use** an atlas, **utilize** both print and electronic encyclopedias, **measure, calculate, select** appropriate materials, and **synthesize** data.

Students then take the information and create an original product whose specifications are satisfied when each glyph direction is followed. The creation of a model, poster or other product is fun and allows for a child's creativity. "<u>GLYPHS</u>" are less involved than full, traditional 'research projects.' Use <u>Researching Adventures → Creating Great "GLYPHS"</u> as an introduction to research before a larger more traditional research project is required. Through glyphs, students will gain valuable practice:

- ✓ Reading for important information
- ✓ Taking notes
- ✓ Organizing data
- ✓ Organizing materials
- ✓ Following directions, and
- ✓ Working with a group to complete a final project

National Educational Standards

While working to complete cross-curricular glyph activities, upper elementary students will gain practice related to many important nationally published educational standards. Standards addressed in Researching Adventures → Creating "GLYPHS" include, but are not limited to, the following statements. (Number order of listing may or may not have been changed from standards as they appear in literature or on web sites.)

English Language Arts Standards addressed are noted as follows, as set by The National Council of Teachers of English.

1. Students read a wide range of print and non-print texts to build an understanding of texts, of themselves, and of the cultures of the United States and the world; to acquire new information...

2. Among these texts are fiction and nonfiction, classic and contemporary works.

3. Students apply a wide range of strategies to comprehend, interpret, evaluate, and appreciate texts. They draw on their prior experience, their interactions with other readers and writers, their knowledge of word meanings and of other texts, their word identification strategies, and their understanding of textual features.

4. Students adjust their use of spoken, written, and visual language...to communicate effectively with a variety of audiences and for different purposes.

5. Students employ a wide range of strategies as they write and appropriately use different writing process elements to communicate with different audiences for a variety of purposes.

6. Students conduct research on issues and interests by generating ideas and questions and by posing problems. They gather, evaluate, and synthesize data from a variety of sources (print and non-print texts, artifacts, people) to communicate their discoveries in ways that suit their purpose and audience.

7. Students use a variety of technological and information resources (libraries, databases, computer networks, video) to gather and synthesize information and to create and communicate knowledge.

8. Students use spoken, written, and visual language to accomplish their own purposes (for learning, enjoyment, persuasion, and the exchange of information.)

Mathematics Standards addressed are noted as follows, taken from The National Council of Teachers of Mathematics.

1. Standard 1: Number and Operation
   - Use computational tools and strategies fluently and estimate appropriately.

2. Standard 2: Patterns, Functions and Algebra
   - Use symbolic forms to represent and analyze mathematical situations and structures.

3. Standard 3: Geometry and Spatial Sense
   - Select and use different representational systems including ... graph theory.
   - Use visualization and spatial reasoning to solve problems both within and outside of mathematics.

4. Standard 4: Measurement
   - Apply a variety of techniques, tools, and formulas for determining measurements.

5. Standard 5: Data Analysis, Statistics and Probability
   - Pose questions and collect, organize, and represent data to answer those questions.
   - Interpret data using methods of exploratory data analysis.

6. Standard 6: Problem Solving
   - Build new mathematical knowledge through their work with problems.
   - Develop a disposition to formulate, represent, abstract, and generalize in situations within and outside mathematics.
   - Apply a wide variety of strategies to solve problems and adapt the strategies to new situations.
   - Monitor and reflect on their mathematical thinking in solving problems.

7. Standard 7: Reasoning and Proof
   - Make and investigate mathematical conjectures.
   - Select and use various types of reasoning and methods of proof as appropriate.

8. Standard 8: Communication
   - Organize and consolidate their mathematical thinking to communicate with others.
   - Express mathematical ideas coherently and clearly to peers, teachers, and others.
   - Extend their mathematical knowledge by considering the thinking and strategies of others.

The Science Standard addressed is stipulated by the National Academy of Sciences.

- Use appropriate tools and techniques to gather, analyze, and interpret data.

Students may also research factual information in science in the areas of
- physical science
- life science
- earth and space science

Social Studies expectations practiced in *Researching Adventures* fall under the area of People, Places and Environments, as published by the National Council for the Social Studies.

    b. Interpret, use, and distinguish various representations of the earth, such as maps, globes, and photographs.

    c. Use appropriate resources, data sources, and geographic tools such as atlases, databases, grid systems, charts, graphs, and maps to generate, manipulate, and interpret information.

    d. Estimate distances and calculate scale.

As you can see from the above standards, many skills students will use to research and problem solve overlap in several areas. Give students the opportunity and encourage them to use available technology during glyph lessons.

Technology Foundation Standards that correlate with Profiles for Technology Literate Students.

1. Basic Operations and Concepts
   - Students are proficient in the use of technology.

2. Social, Ethical, and Human Issues
   - Students practice responsible use of technology systems, information, and software.
   - Students develop positive attitudes toward technology uses that support lifelong learning, collaboration, personal pursuits, and productivity.

3. Technology Productivity Tools
   - Students use technology tools to enhance learning, increase productivity, and promote creativity.

4. Technology Communication Tools
    - Students use telecommunications to collaborate, publish, and interact with peers, experts, and other audiences.

5. Technology Research Tools
    - Students use technology to locate, evaluate, and collect information from a variety of sources.
    - Students evaluate and select new information resources and technological innovations based on appropriateness of the specific task.

Web sites current as of 7/1/2004
Standards for the English Language Arts, p.24, 1996, International Reading Association and National Council of Teachers of English. (*http://www.ncte.org/*)

Principles and Standards for School Mathematics: Discussion Draft, October 1996, National Council of Teachers of Mathematics. (*http://www.nctm.org*)

National Science Education Standards, 1996, National Academy of Sciences, National Academy Press, Washington D.C. (*http://www.nap.edu/readingroom/books/nses/html*)

Expectations of Excellence: curriculum Standards for Social Studies, 1994, National Council for the Social Studies, NCSS Publications. (*http://www.socialstudies.org/standards/* or *http://www.ncss.org*)

Technology Foundation Standards for Students, National Educational Technology Standards (NETS) for Students. International Society for Technology in Education (ISTE.) (*http://cnets.iste.org/currstands/cstands-netss.html*)

Getting Started

When do I use glyphs?

Individuals or small groups can complete glyphs. These activities are valuable in a resource classroom as well as in the regular classroom. Use glyph activities
- when students have compacted out of the regular curriculum
- as learning center activities

Glyphs pull from many subject areas, but each glyph stresses one skill area over the other areas. The book is organized by these strengths. Choose from

* Language Arts   * Math
* Science   * Social Studies

How do I get started?

The first time you introduce glyphs, you may want to pull small groups of students and model for them using the 'think aloud' strategy. Show students how to use the GLYPH Research Checklist (optional page 73) to guide their research efforts and discuss with them how to organize their notes. Then, establish which student or student group will be completing a glyph. Choose an appropriate glyph based upon its subject strength, or let the student(s) choose. Provide the student(s) with a copy of the one-page glyph directions and a file or pocket folder. Students may use the folder to store the glyph directions and research notes.

Materials

On the teacher direction page preceding each new glyph direction is a suggested *Research Materials* list. It is a starting point and not meant to be exclusive. (Other materials – art supplies like construction paper, markers, crayons, glue, scissors, etc. are not listed.) Your students may use any research materials that provide accurate information for which they are looking. You may wish to suggest specific web sites or electronic encyclopedias or allow students to use a school intranet. This will increase the chance that students gain access to accurate information from reliable sources. Encourage students to use at least **three** different sources to verify information as they complete each glyph.

Time Line

The time needed to complete a glyph depends on several factors. Time will vary from one glyph to the next based on a student's prior knowledge of a particular subject. A student's level of research savvy and note-taking skills will also play a role in how quickly a glyph is completed. Take into consideration whether a student is working alone or in a small group.

Assign work segments for a glyph for no less than 30 minutes. This will allow for positive progress to be made. As students become more proficient and experienced with glyphs, you may reduce the minimum time. Most students can complete a glyph in 3-5 segments.

© Pieces of Learning

Teacher Tips

- Use the practice pages for research from an almanac, atlas and encyclopedia. These sheets are located in the Appendix (pages 73 –79). These pages will help students learn how to navigate these tools and be better familiar with the information each one offers.

- Have art supplies easily accessible. Students will then be able to construct the glyph individually or in their small groups without interrupting other classroom instruction.

- Provide students with the GLYPH Research Checklist (page 73) and encourage them to use it.

- Post the research tips that are listed on the GLYPH Research Checklist in the classroom. You might also staple a copy of them to the student's work folder.

- Students do not have to research the items in order. As long as they take quality notes and organize the findings, they will be able to pull together what they have learned. However, the first direction on the page is usually key to the overall project. Have them check the line when they have completed a task.

- Have students collect all data before any construction of the product is started.

Apple GLYPH
Early Elementary Example

In the early elementary grades, GLYPHS are very basic, very short. They involve facts about a child's physical or family characteristics and personal likes and dislikes.

Directions are simple. All pieces needed to construct the glyph would be precut for the children so all that is required of them is decision making and assembly. They do not allow for a lot of creativity on the students' part. Directions are usually displayed on large chart paper and would have a picture of each piece to be used next to each corresponding direction to assist early readers.

For Example:

___ 1. If you are a boy = choose a red apple.
___   If you are a girl = choose a green apple.

___ 2. If you were born in Georgia = choose a black stem
___   If you were not born in Georgia = choose a brown stem

___ 3. Put one green leaf on the stem for every brother or sister you have.

___ 4. Add a pink worm = you like READING the best at school.
___   Add a yellow worm = you like MATH the best at school.

© Pieces of Learning

Apple GLYPH
Example

Glyphs that follow go beyond requiring simple, personal knowledge. Each statement or question on the GLYPH direction page will require students to research. When they have completed all clues they will know how to complete their assignment. A partial example of a GLYPH activity is on page 15.

The MONSTER of NICE GLYPH
Sample Directions

Follow the directions to create a model of the Monster of Nice. Use print and on-line sources for your research. Take notes. Be sure to read through all the clues before you begin. Good luck!

___ 1. If the city of Nice is in the Old World – make your monster 12" tall.
___   If it is in the New World – make the monster 6" tall.

___ 2. If the monster of Nice lives near the water – make the body blue.
___   If it lives inland – make the body green.

___ 3. If the population of Nice is below 50,000 – make the monster have yellow spots.
___   If the population is greater than 50,000 – make the monster have purple spots.

___ 4. If the monster is 100 miles or less from the Eiffel Tower – give him one eye.
___   If he is more than 100 miles from that landmark – give him two eyes.

When beginning to research each item, it is helpful if students learn to highlight important words in each clue. They can use the GLYPH Research Checklist (found in the Appendix) to help track which reference materials they use. After completing the entire list of clues, students will construct the monster. They are encouraged to reread the clues and make sure their monster is the true *Monster of Nice*. Students add details to the finished monster. The color of eyes, for example, is not specified. Students may use their creativity to color the monster and add extra elements, as long as it does not take away or change required elements.

© Pieces of Learning

Language Arts
GLYPHS

- Cereal GLYPH   p. 17
- Octopus GLYPH   p. 20
- Candy Bar GLYPH   p. 23
- "Good Morning" Soda GLYPH p. 26
- Flag GLYPH   p. 29

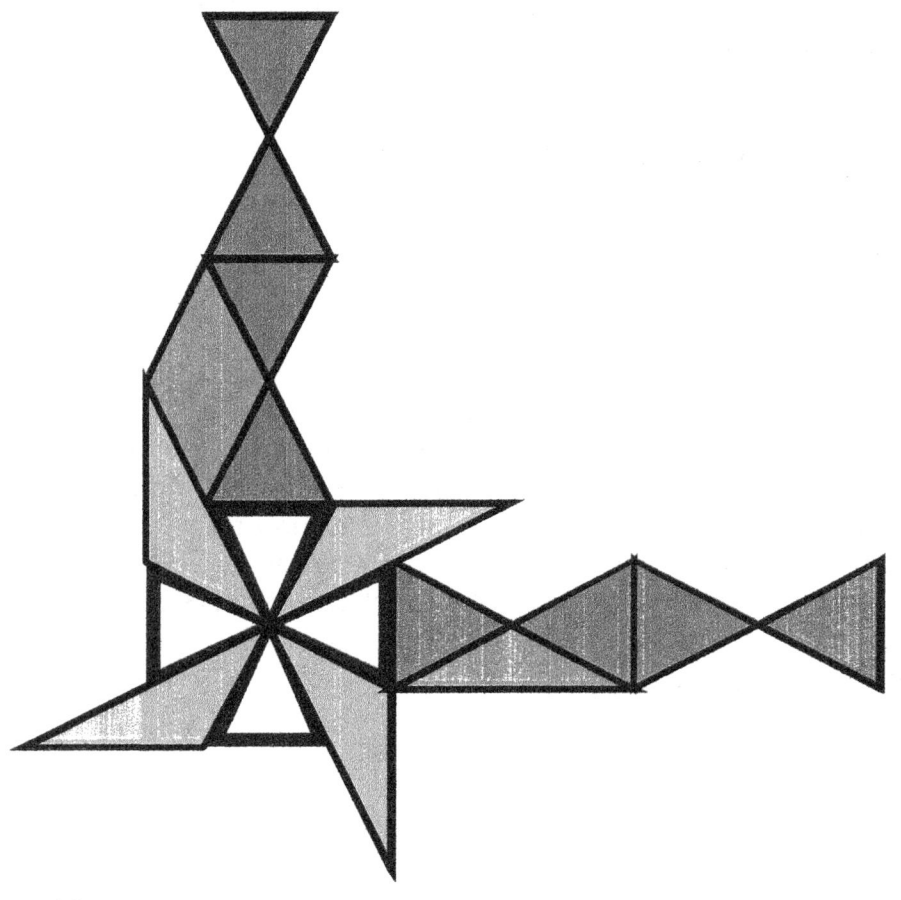

Directions for the Teacher

Cereal GLYPH

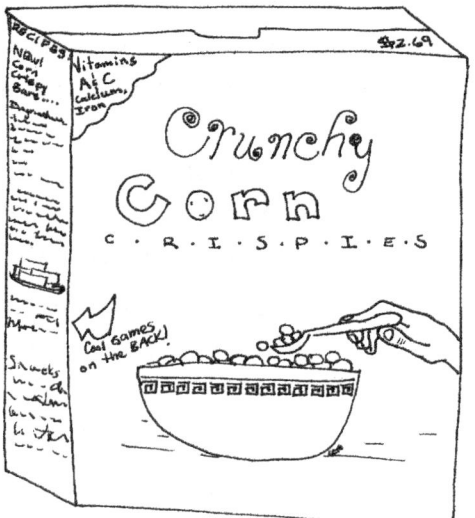

Focus Skill: The focus skill of this glyph is **language**.

Insight Gained: Students will explore new vocabulary and familiar **math skills**. They will work creatively, noticing and repeating **advertising techniques** aimed at children to create a model of a new cereal.

Research Materials:
- Dictionary
- Encyclopedias (print and/or electronic)
- Human Resources
- The Internet
- Newspaper grocery advertisements and coupons
- Non-fiction books on Greece, Greek fine-arts, or jewelry catalogs

Answer Key:

The finished model should be an empty cereal box covered in craft paper. The color was not specified. All designs should be drawn directly on the box or affixed to it in some way.

1. Maize is another name for corn. The title of the cereal should have corn in it, and may contain an additional descriptive word, (Corn Crispies for example.) The title should be written in the top third of the box front.
2. A bowl bearing a Greek key design should be pictured on the bottom third of the box front. The Greek key design has horizontal, interlocking, elongated L shapes.
3. The bowl should have pictures of orb shaped (spherical) cereal in it.
4. On a triangle in the NW corner of the box front, students could have listed Vitamin A, C, and Minerals.
5. The search-a-word on the back should contain words from a mechanic's vocabulary, like engine, carburetor, gasket, filter, gas, hoses, alternator.
6. Check the recipe on a thin side of the box to see that it has the ingredients, directions, and a picture of the suggested snack food.
7. The cashier would give $2.31 in change from a $5 bill, so the cereal costs $2.69. This price should be written on the top flap.

There are no specifications for the second thin side of the box. Students may be creative and add coupons, more games, or other information there.

© Pieces of Learning

Cereal GLYPH

Follow the directions to create a model of a box of a new cereal that is ready to hit the market shelves! In order to complete the box, start with an empty cereal box covered with craft paper and follow the steps below. Collect all information necessary to make an accurate model of the new cereal. Be creative with your choice of paper color and lettering styles.

____ 1. The grain that your cereal is made of is called *maize*, but most people know it by another name. Use the more common name in the title of the cereal. You may add a descriptive word to it like crispies, crunchies, etc. Write this name prominently in the top 1/3 of the front of the box.

____ 2. Draw a cereal bowl on the bottom third of the box front. Make the cereal bowl have a Greek key design across the top.

____ 3. The cereal is shaped like small orbs. Draw the cereal heaped in the bowl. Add a pewter-colored spoon.

____ 4. Most cereal boxes advertise they contain important vitamins and minerals. Find out three of the most common vitamins and minerals with which cereals are fortified. Write their names on a triangular piece of paper. Attach it to the NW corner of the front of the box.

____ 5. Cereal aimed at children usually has games and puzzles on the back of the box. Make a search-a-word for the back of your model. Hide at least 10 words in your puzzle. Use words that would be in a mechanic's vocabulary.

____ 6. On one thin side of the box, suggest a recipe that could be made with this cereal. It could be a cold snack or a baked treat. Be sure to include the ingredients, preparation directions, and a picture of the finished treat.

____ 7. If someone purchased this cereal and paid with a $5 bill, the cashier would give the following change: 2 dollar bills, 1 quarter, 1 nickel and 1 penny. What is the price of the cereal? Write the price on the top flap of the cereal box.

Sample Answer – Cereal Box

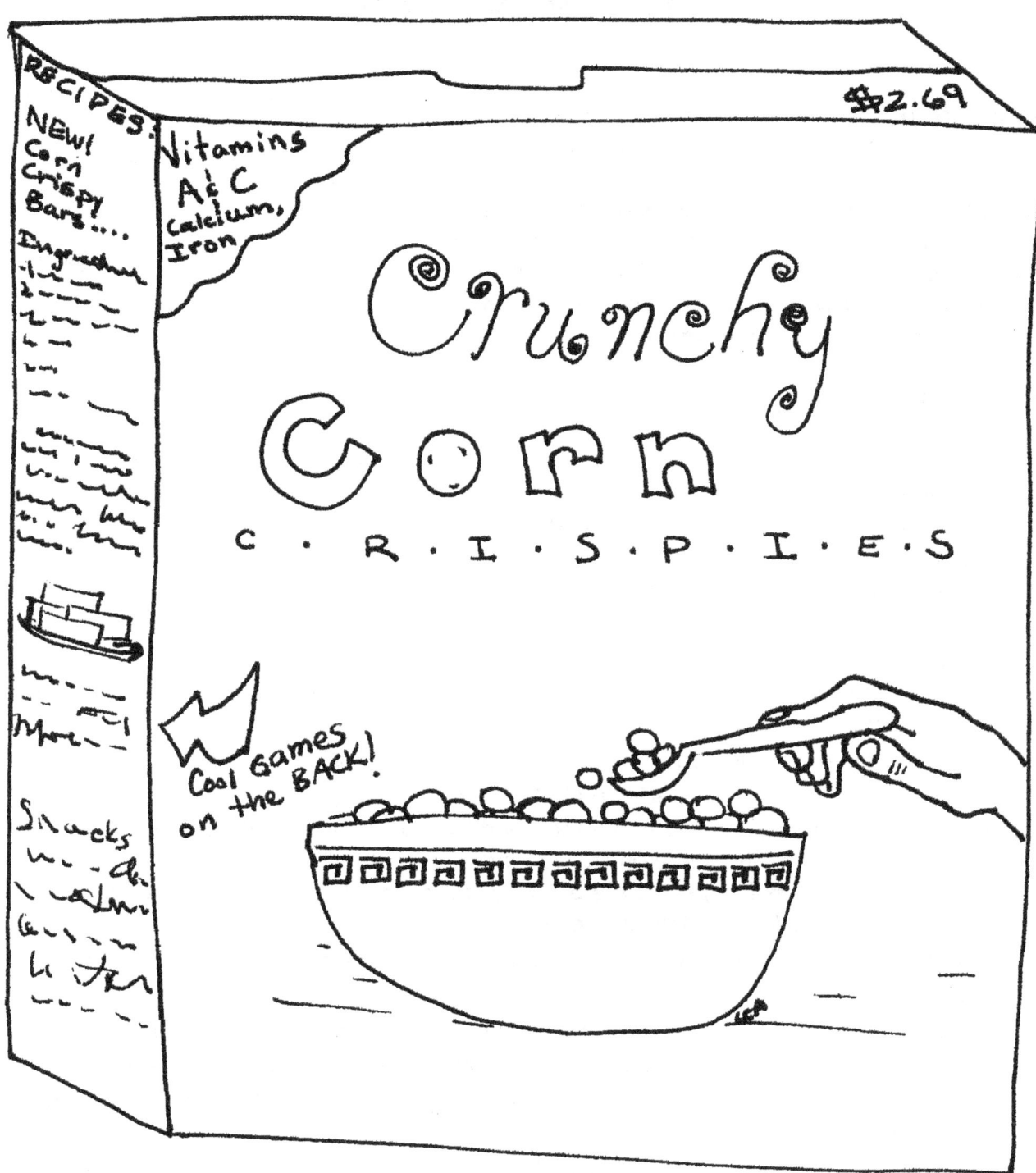

Directions for the Teacher

Octopus GLYPH

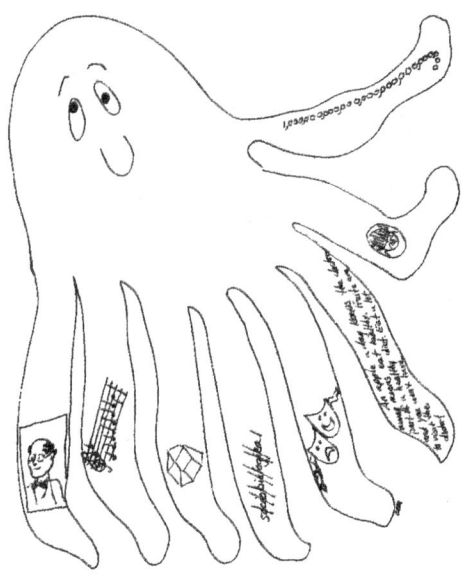

Focus Skill: The focus skill of this glyph is **language/word meanings.**

Insight Gained: Students will need to use their **dictionary skills** to search for and analyze word **meanings**. They will also research aspects of two **ancient civilizations** and look into a common phrase of the English **language**.

Research Materials:
- Dictionary
- Encyclopedias (print and or electronic)
- The Internet
- Non-fiction texts about ancient Greece and Egypt
- Non-fiction text about music theory

Answer Key:
The octopus should be either 12" or 14" across on a shade of blue, green or purple paper. (cool colors)

1. An octogenarian is a person who is 80 years old. The first arm on the left should have a picture of a person approximately that age.
2. An octave is the interval between a tone and the same tone eight degrees from it. An image of a scale should be on the second arm. It should start on b flat and continue up the staff- **b flat, c, d, e flat, f, g, a, b flat**. Preferably the students would also have a *b* and *e flat* in the key signature.
3. An octahedron is a solid figure with eight faces. A 3-dimensional model should appear on the third arm.
4. Answers will vary. Students should record an eight syllable word on the fourth arm of the octopus. Possible answers are sociobiological and histocompatability.
5. Students should have a 1"-2" mask of comedy (grin) and tragedy (frown) faces attached to the fifth arm.
6. An apple a day keeps the doctor away. Students should have 2-3 sentences explaining what they think that saying means.
7. An image of a scarab (beetle) should appear on the seventh arm.
8. In the U.S. and France an octillion is a cardinal number with 1- followed by 27 zeros. (In Great Britain and Germany, it is 1- followed by 48 zeros.)

Octopus GLYPH

Follow the directions to create a paper or tag board octopus. Choose a cool color. Make its length in inches an even number greater than 10 but less than 16. Research the following information using print and on-line sources. Take notes. You will add a corresponding picture or image to each of the legs on the octopus. Use original art or clip art from periodicals or non-copyrighted Internet sources.

___ 1. What is an *octogenarian*? Put a picture of one on the first arm of the octopus, starting on the left.

___ 2. What is an *octave*? Draw a diagram of one. Start at *b flat*. Place it on the second arm.

___ 3. What is an *octahedron*? Make one out of white paper and attach it to the third arm.

___ 4. Find a word that is *octosyllabic*. Write it on the fourth arm.

___ 5. The ancient Greeks were the first to perform plays and developed the styles of comedy and tragedy. Actors wore masks with exaggerated faces. Find out how comedy and tragedy are usually depicted on masks together. Make small (1"-2") versions of the masks and affix them to the fifth arm.

___ 6. Finish the saying "An apple a day..." Why do you suppose someone would say that? On the sixth octopus arm write a few sentences about your opinion.

___ 7. Ancient Egyptians put a carved amulet over a mummy's heart. What was this sacred gem called? What was it carved to look like? Put a picture of one on the seventh arm.

___ 8. To what is an *octillion* equal? Write its amount as it would appear in the U.S. and France on the eighth arm of the octopus.

Re-read the questions and be sure your octopus displays the correct images. Be creative and add other details to the sea creature.

© Pieces of Learning

Sample Answer Octopus Glyph

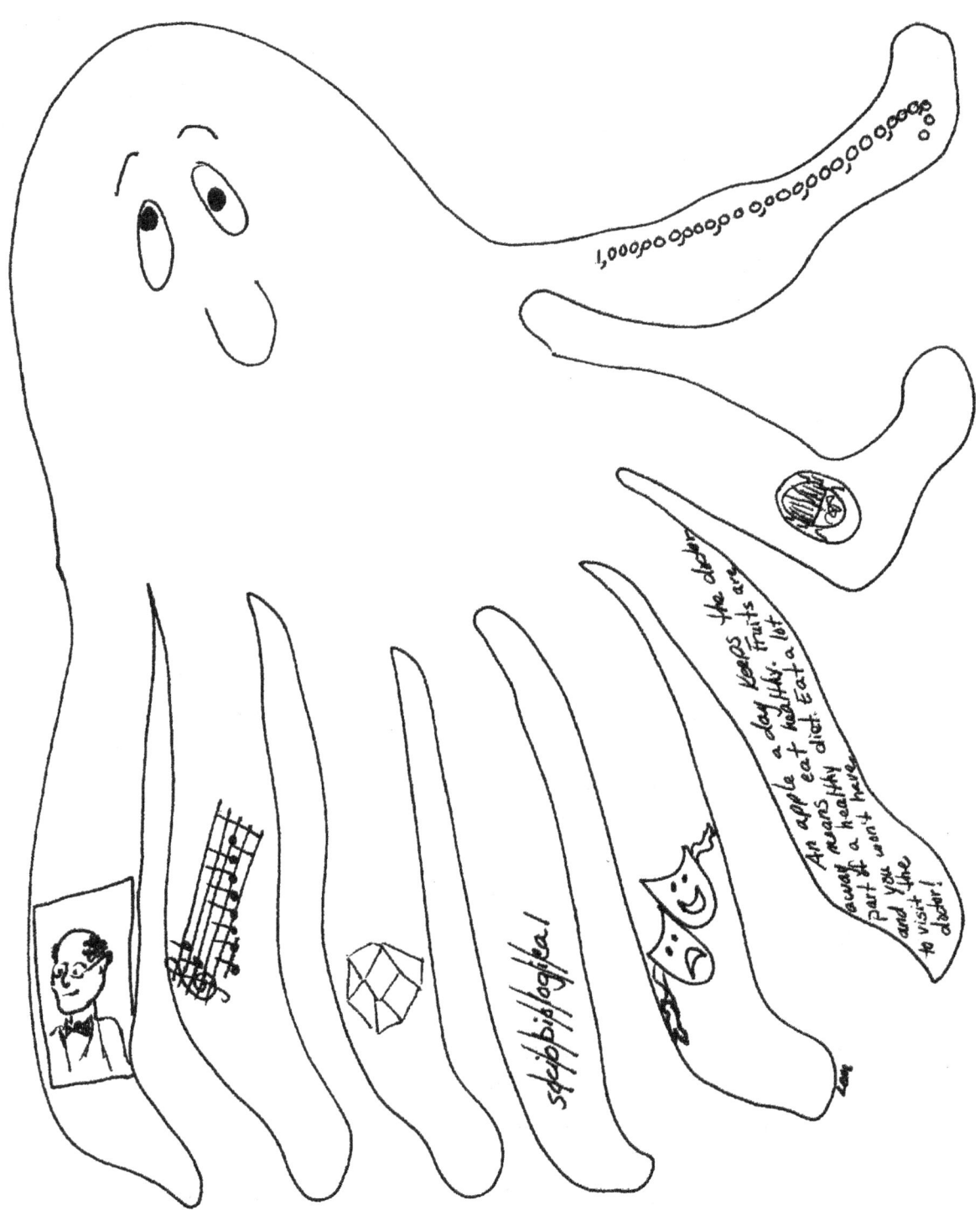

Directions for the Teacher

Candy Bar GLYPH

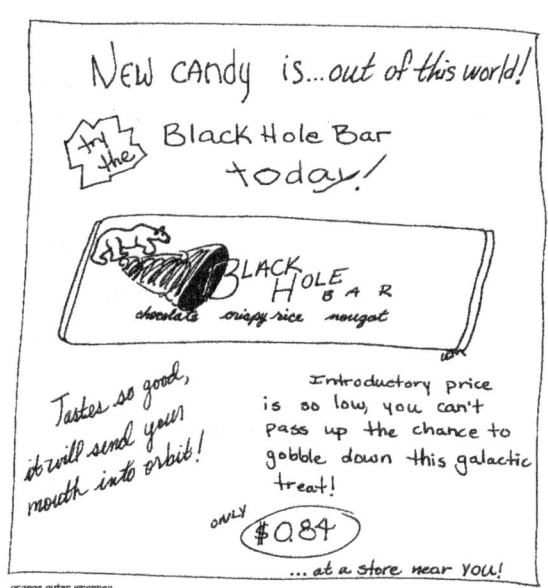

Focus Skill: The focus skill of this glyph is **language**.

Insight Gained: Students will be able to show their **creativity** both artistically and visually. **Math, science** and **social studies skills** will also be used.

Research Materials:
- Almanac
- Dictionary
- Encyclopedias (print and/or electronic)
- The Internet
- Non-fiction texts about the solar system

Answer Key:

The candy bar will appear in the center of an advertisement. The bar may be a 3-dimensional model attached to the ad, or it may be drawn directly on the ad.

1. Oscar the Grouch was originally orange. The outer candy wrapper should be orange.

2. Students may name the candy bar any name that is associated with astronomy.

3. It should be creatively written on the outer wrapper.

4. The ingredients unscrambled should be written below the name of the candy bar on the outer wrapper. They are: chocolate, crispy rice and nougat.

5. The polar bear lives 20 years, so the image of the bear should appear left of the title of the candy bar.

6. No less than three selling points should be written around the candy bar on the advertisement. Check for rich adjectives and fully edited sentences that are reasonable statements about the merits of a candy bar.

7. There are 8 quarts in a peck and 4 pecks in a bushel. The cost of the candy bar written on the ad is $0.84.

Students may add other creative details to their advertisement. Look for novel ideas, varied color, elaboration and an overall pleasing advertisement.

© Pieces of Learning

Candy Bar GLYPH

Follow the directions to create the advertisement for a new, original candy bar. You may make a model of the new candy bar by covering a long jewelry type box (2" x 6") with paper, or you may simply draw the bar on the advertising sign. Research the following information using print and on-line sources.

___ 1. For the outer wrapper of the new candy bar, use paper that is the same as the original color of fur for Oscar the Grouch.
     orange   green   light blue   yellow   turquoise

___ 2. Some candy bars have astronomical names (Mars, Milky Way.) Choose a name for this candy bar that comes from astronomy.

___ 3. Write the name creatively across the front of the wrapper.

___ 4. Unscramble the following ingredient words and write them on the wrapper below the name of the candy bar.
     heclotoca   ripycs cier   tonuga

___ 5. Which of these animals has the longest life span? Use a picture of that animal on your candy bar on the west side of the name.
     polar bear   rabbit   Great Dane

___ 6. On the advertising sign, surround the candy bar with advertising selling points. What makes this candy bar special? Why should someone buy it? Write at least three selling points on the advertisement. Use expressive language and edit fully.

___ 7. Include the price of the candy bar on the advertisement. Follow the steps to get the correct amount: How many quarts are in a peck? Use this number in the tens place. How many pecks are in a bushel? Use this number in the ones place.

Re-read the clues and check your model to be sure your new candy is market ready.

© Pieces of Learning

Sample Answer Candy Bar Glyph

New candy is...out of this world!

try the Black Hole Bar today!

Black Hole Bar
chocolate   crispy rice   nougat

Tastes so good, it will send your mouth into orbit!

Introductory price is so low, you can't pass up the chance to gobble down this galactic treat!

ONLY $0.84

...at a store near you!

orange outer wrapper

© Pieces of Learning

Directions for the Teacher

"Good Morning" Soda GLYPH

Focus Skill: The focus skill of this glyph is **language**.

Insight Gained: Students will need to explore **foreign languages**, work by a popular **children's author**, and **literature awards**. They will also research in the areas of **geography** and **science**.

Research Materials:
- Dictionary
- Encyclopedias (print and/or electronic)
- French to English dictionary
- The Internet
- Non-fiction texts about science, anatomy
- Ruler
- Spanish to English dictionary

Answer Key:

Students should cover an empty, washed soda can for their model.

1. Three languages should be used on the can label (see #5), Good Morning, Buenos Dias (Spanish) and Bonjour (French).

2. The label will be yellow, as caffeine stimulates the central nervous system and increases blood pressure.

3. The atomic number of Helium is 2. One hundred x 2= 200 calories.

4. Chris Van Allsburg includes a white (terrier) dog in his illustrations. A picture of the dog should be on the can label. (Somewhat hidden in many books, it is a main character in *The Garden of Abdul Gasazi.)*

5. The Caldecott award is given for illustrations, so the name of the soda (in all three languages) should be written vertically on the label.

6. An example bar code should be on the can with the numbers 21105 underneath the bars. King Tut was 9 when he became king of Egypt. Nine x 2,345= 21105.

"Good Morning" Soda GLYPH

There's a new kind of soda pop entering the market. Cover an empty, clean soda can with craft paper and follow the directions to decorate a model of the new ..."Good Morning" beverage, *guaranteed to wake you with a blink*!

___ 1. *Good Morning* soda will be sold in the United States, Mexico City and Quebec. Find out how people would say the name *Good Morning* in these locations. Use any and all appropriate languages on the can label.

___ 2. This soda contains caffeine. If caffeine helps wake you up because it stimulates the central nervous system, make the can label yellow. If caffeine wakes you up because it stimulates the circulatory system, make the can label orange.

___ 3. The number of calories in *Good Morning* is equal to 100 times the atomic number of Helium. Put this number on the can telling consumers how many calories they are drinking.

___ 4. What animal is illustrated in every Chris Van Allsburg book? Put a picture of this animal on the soda label.

___ 5. Which award is given for the illustrations in children's books? If it is the Caldecott, write the name of the soda (in all appropriate languages) vertically on the can label. If it is the Newbery, write the names horizontally on the label.

___ 6. Draw a bar code on the can. Make the numbers that appear below the series of lines (or bars) 2,345 times greater than the age of King Tutankhamen when he became the king of Egypt.

Follow all the steps above to create a model of the new *Good Morning* soda drink. Work neatly and creatively as you put information on the label.

Sample Answer Soda Glyph

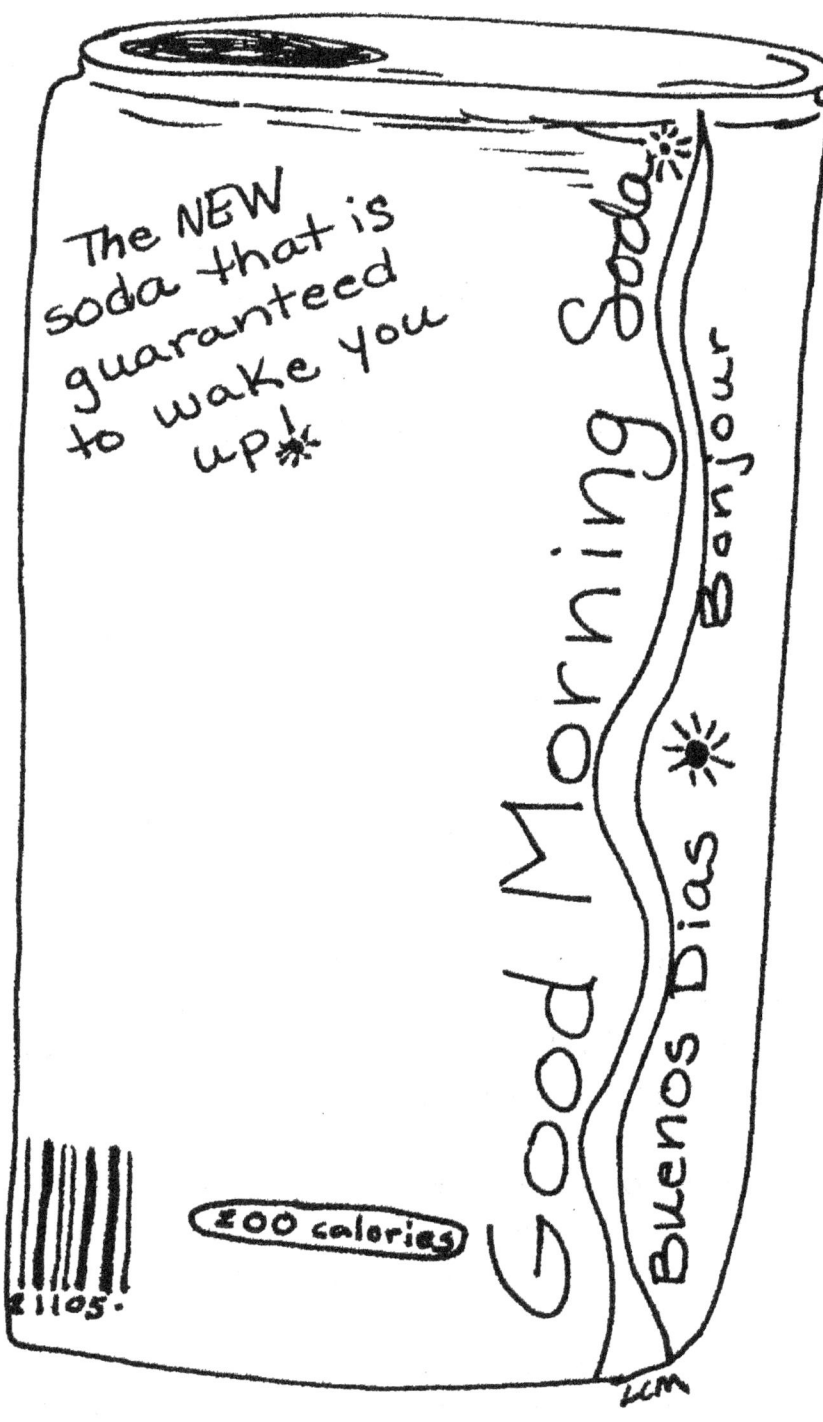

yellow label

Directions for the Teacher

Flag GLYPH

Focus Skill: The focus skill of this glyph is **literature/language arts**.

Insight Gained: Students will need to research well-known **literary works** to learn information about **main characters**. They will also use **measurement skills** to correctly identify the dimensions of the flag and pole.

Research Materials:
- Encyclopedias (print and/or electronic)
- The Internet
- Literary works (Runaway Ralph, Little Women, The Glass Menagerie, The Wind in the Willows and The Hobbit)
- Ruler or tape measure

Answer Key:

Students should have a paper or felt flag.

1. The flag is red, because Ralph's motorcycle is red.

2. Answers will vary, but lengths will probably be around 12", and the height of the flag should be at least 2/3 of that (8").

3. Evenly spaced along the bottom edge there should be four smiley faces, each labeled with a name - Meg, Jo, Beth and Amy. The color of the faces is not specified. They could be all the same or a variety of colors.

4. There should be a unicorn in the NW corner of the flag.

5. The center of the flag should have four 3" pictures, one each of a toad, badger, rat and a mole.

6. The Hobbit's real name is Bilbo Baggins, so the flag pole should be 16" tall.

© Pieces of Learning

Flag GLYPH

Follow the directions below to create an original flag. Use several different resources for your research. Take careful notes. Be sure to read through all the clues before you begin. Have fun!

___ 1. Use paper or felt for the flag. The color should be the same color as Ralph's motorcycle in *The Mouse and the Motorcycle.*

___ 2. Cut a rectangle that is the same length in inches as the distance from your elbow to your finger tips. Make the height at least 2/3 of the length. This is the background of your flag.

___ 3. Along the bottom edge of the flag, put one smiley face for each of the sisters in *Little Women*. Evenly space out the faces. Write the name of a sister underneath each face.

___ 4. In the play *The Glass Menagerie*, the main character Laura treasures a favorite item. What is this item? Put a 4" picture of it in the NW corner of the flag.

___ 5. Make several 3" tall pictures of the main animal characters from *The Wind in the Willows*. Arrange them in the center of the flag.

___ 6. Who is also known as *The Hobbit?* Select cardboard or tag board according to the lengths below. This is the flag pole to which you will attach the flag.

    Smaug- 14"   Bilbo Baggins- 16"   Gandolf-18"

Construct your new flag. Re-read the clues and be sure you include all necessary elements. Be creative and colorful.

Math
GLYPHS

- Mystery Number GLYPH   p. 32
- Wrist Watch GLYPH   p. 34
- Great Dessert GLYPH   p. 37
- Computer GLYPH   p. 39
- Flag II GLYPH   p. 41

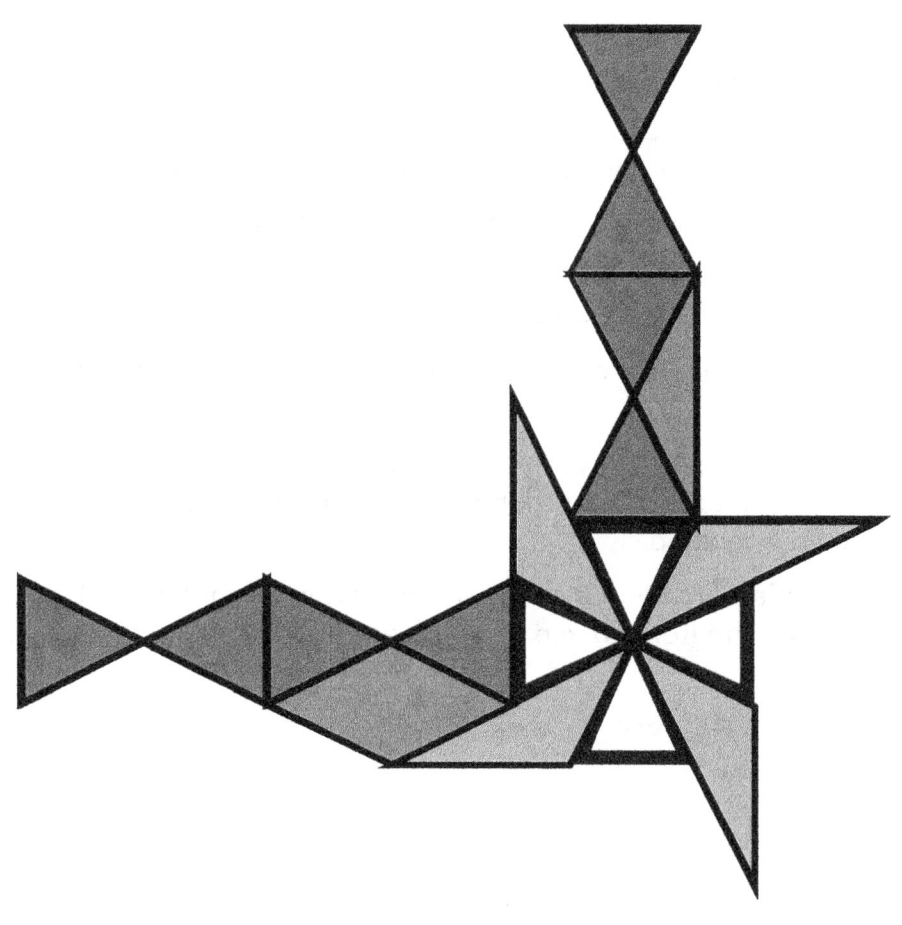

Directions for the Teacher

Mystery Number GLYPH

Focus Skill: The focus skill of this glyph is **math**.

Insight Gained: Although requiring students to do several **calculations**, they will also first examine their own and/or group members' ages, **U.S. history**, and **U.S. geography**.

Research Materials:
- Almanac
- Atlas
- Calculator
- Dictionary
- Encyclopedias (print and/or electronic)
- The Internet
- Non-fiction texts about Maine (provided only after students discover clue #5 leads them to Maine.)

Answer Key:

1. Answers will vary. Example- student A is 9.2 years old = 110 months, and even number. Paper should be blue. Odd numbers will have green paper.

2. Answers will vary. Ages equally divisible by 2 = model is 6" tall. If not model is 8" tall.

3. Benjamin Harrison was 23rd president. The mystery number is 23.

4. Twenty-three is a prime number, therefore the model of 23 should have black dots on it.

5. Maine was the 23rd state to join the United States. The model of number 23 should be mounted on paper that is the outline of the state of Maine. The background color is not specified.

6. Maine's primary industries are timber, sand, gravel and fish. Accept any of these as long as the item affixed is 3" tall and set in the southwest corner of the number model.

7. Answers will vary.

Mystery Number GLYPH

Follow the directions to create a model of the mystery number. Use print and on-line sources for your research. Take notes. Be sure to read through all the clues before you begin. Good luck!

___ 1. Determine how old you are in <u>months</u>. If this number is an even number, use blue paper for the model cut-out of the mystery number. Use green paper for an odd number. (If you are working with a group, take the sum of your ages in months.)

___ 2. If your age in <u>years</u> is equally divisible by 2, make the model 6" tall. If it is not divisible by 2, make it 8" tall. (Again, if you are working in a group, use the sum of your ages and decide if it is even or odd.)

___ 3. The mystery number is equal to the presidential term held by Benjamin Harrison. (B. Harrison was our _____ president.)

___ 4. If this number is a prime number add black dots to the model.

___ 5. Mount the mystery number on a piece of paper that is the same shape as the outline of the state whose addition to the United States shares the same number as the mystery number.
For example: If Harrison was our 50th president, then you would mount the mystery number on paper cut like the outline of Hawaii, since Hawaii was the 50th state added to the union.

___ 6. Make a 3" picture of the main industry of that state and attach it to the southwest corner of the mystery number.

___ 7. If you (or any member of your group) have ever visited this state, draw a yellow star on the number. If your teacher has visited this state, put a ring around the star.

Construct a paper model of the mystery number. Re-read the clues and make sure that you got the right number.

© Pieces of Learning

Directions for the Teacher

Wrist Watch GLYPH

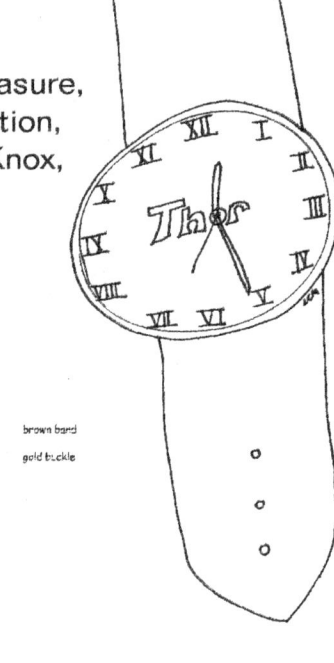

Focus Skill: The focus skill of this glyph is **math**.

Insight Gained: Students will use **mathematical skills** to measure, convert feet to miles and correctly write Roman numerals. In addition, they will find out how Thursday got its name, what is kept at Ft. Knox, and read an old nursery rhyme.

Research Materials:
- Almanac
- Dictionary
- Encyclopedias (print and/or electronic)
- Geometry text
- The Internet
- Non-fiction texts about mythology
- Nursery Rhyme books
- Ruler

Answer Key:

The students should complete a drawing of a wrist watch. Size of finished drawing is not specified other than the size of the watch face (see #1 below). However, the watch band should be proportional.

1. Diameter is twice the radius. A radius of 2 ½ = a circular face that is 5" across.

2. The watch band should be brown and 3" wide. Length of the band is not specified.

3. King Cole had three fiddlers, so one side of the band should have 3 holes. The other side should have a gold colored buckle since gold is kept at Ft. Knox.

4. Roman numerals 1-12 should appear correctly and neatly spaced out on the watch face.

5. Thursday was named for Thor, so his name should appear in the center of the watch face.

6. Three miles is equal to 15,840 feet, so the watch should have an hour, minute, and second hand. Color is not given for the hands.

Wrist Watch GLYPH

Make a rendering of a watch. Follow the directions below. Use print and on-line sources to find the information you need. Take notes and double check your calculations.

___ 1. The face of the watch will be a circle and have a radius of 2 ½ inches.

___ 2. The watch band will be 3" wide. To find out the appropriate color, find out what word in geometry that describes angles has a meaning outside of geometry that means *strange or odd*.
    acute - make the watch band black
    obtuse - make the band brown

___ 3. Show holes in one side of the band for the buckle. Put the number of holes equal to the number of fiddlers Old King Cole had in the nursery rhyme.

___ 4. Add a buckle to the other side of the band. The color of the buckle should match the material that is stored at Ft. Knox.

___ 5. Write Roman numerals on the watch face clearly and correctly spaced.

___ 6. In the center of the face, write the name from mythology for whom Thursday was named.

___ 7. Your watch should have hands. Find out how many miles are equivalent to 15,840 feet.
    Two miles = make an hour and minute hand
    Three miles = make an hour, minute, and second hand

Be sure to collect all needed information and include what is necessary on the watch. Be creative. Add texture to the watch band, and make the hands colorful.

Sample Wrist Watch Glyph

brown band

gold buckle

Directions for the Teacher

Great Dessert GLYPH

Focus Skill: The focus skill of this glyph is **math**.

Insight Gained: The math skills used in this glyph are varied from mathematical terminology to division. Students will also learn new **vocabulary** and look up a **stock** in the newspaper.

Research Materials:
- Atlas
- Dictionary
- The Internet
- Ruler
- Newspaper
- Upper level math book, or mathematical dictionary

Answer Key:

1. The Great Dessert is a pie. (The principle 3.14 is *pi*.)

2. The pie must be shown from above. It is 183 mi. from Wichita to Kansas City. Multiply 183 x 1.6 to get the distance in kilometers. This equals 292.80 km, divided by 13=22.5. The diameter of the base crust should be 22.5 cm. It should be cut from tan paper and glued to the center of the poster.

3. The Great Dessert is a Key Lime pie. The filling should be shown with light green paper or paint directly on top of the bottom crust.

4. Tan paper strips should be made in the lattice pattern (over, under, over, under in both directions) and glued over the filling.

5. The white price tag may be a 5 cm square, rectangle or diamond shape (any parallelogram.) The price of Coca Cola will vary, however, the current price is divided by 10 to obtain the cost of the pie. (For example, $54 a share divided by 10= $5.40 for the pie.)

6. There are 16 oz. in a pound. Sixteen x 2 pounds = 32 ounces divided by 8 people is 4 ounces per serving. This number should appear in the center of the pie.

No background color or size for the poster was specified, however 12" x 18" was suggested. Students were encouraged to add details to the poster like a place mat or utensils.

© Pieces of Learning

Great Dessert GLYPH

Follow the directions to create a poster of a great dessert. Use print and on-line sources for your research. Take notes. Be sure to read through all the clues before you begin. Good luck!

___ 1. The name of the dessert is a homophone. To see what it is, find out what mathematical principle is equal to 3.14.

___ 2. Show the dessert on your poster from a bird's eye view. Find the distance in miles from Wichita to Kansas City. Convert this number to kilometers. Now divide by 13. Measure this number in cm for the diameter of the dessert.

___ 3. Color the filling. The filling is a fruit. This famous dessert hails from Key West, Florida.

___ 4. Make a lattice top crust out of tan paper and glue it on top of the colored filling on your poster.

___ 5. Affix a price tag. For the price, divide the price of one share of Coca Cola stock by 10.

___ 6. If the dessert weighs 3 lbs. excluding the dish, and 8 people share it evenly, what is the serving size per person in ounces? Write this number in the center of the dessert.

Be creative and add details to the drawing, such as a placemat or utensils. A good size for your poster is 12" x 18" so the dessert can be realistically sized. You may also wish to layer paper with drawn elements to make your poster *relief.*

Directions for the Teacher

Computer GLYPH

Focus Skill: The focus skill of this glyph is **math**.

Insight Gained: They will practice skills in **math** as well as **science** and **social studies**. Students will be able to show their **creativity**.

Research Materials:
- Almanac
- Dictionary
- Encyclopedias (print and/or electronic)
- The Internet
- Math texts
- Non-fiction texts about Henry Ford, Ford Motor Co., or cars

Answer Key:

The computer should be a model constructed from cardboard or tag board covered in paper. Students may try to make the monitor vertical, or they may leave it flat.

1. There is a Monitor lizard, so the screen should be light blue.

2. The Sears Tower has 110 stories, divided by 4= 27.5. The square screen should be 27.5 cm on each side, or students may round to 28cm.

3. The first Ford car was black, so the background frame for the screen should be black. It should also stick out from behind the screen 1½ in. on all sides.

4. Three lines of binary code should be written on the monitor screen. Accept any logical sequence of code (100100011111010010, etc.)

5. The keyboard should also be cardboard and should have all the keys represented and labeled from a standard computer keyboard.

6. Hurricane force winds are stronger than gale force winds, so the *escape* key should be colored red.

7. The difference between hurricane (80 mph) and gale force winds (40 mph) is greater than 20. The **!** key should be colored orange.

8. "Southpaws" would prefer the mouse on the left side of the keyboard. Students should have the mouse attached with yarn or string.

© Pieces of Learning

Computer GLYPH

Make a model of a computer monitor. Use cardboard or tag board, cover it with craft paper, and follow the directions to decorate your model.

___ 1. Start by making the square monitor for your computer. Choose the color for the monitor by finding the answer to this question: Which animal has a variety called 'Monitor?'
*eagle- gray paper   *lizard- light blue paper   *catfish- royal blue paper

___ 2. Cut the appropriate paper into a square. To find length and width, divide the number of stories in the Sears Tower by 4. Use this number in centimeters. Round the number to the nearest whole number.

___ 3. The monitor should be placed on a background so that exactly 1½ inches frames it on all sides. Make the background the same color as the first Ford car ever manufactured.

___ 4. Place three lines of binary code on the monitor screen.

___ 5. On another piece of cardboard, draw a representation on a computer keyboard. Be sure to include all keys and label them.

___ 6. If hurricane force winds are stronger than gale force winds, color the *escape* key red. If gale force winds are stronger than a hurricane's winds, color the *escape* key green.

___ 7. If the difference between the average hurricane's winds and gale force winds is less than 20, color the **!** key yellow. If the difference between their averages is greater than 20, color the **!** key orange.

___ 8. Make a mouse for your computer and attach it to the keyboard with yarn or string. Attach the mouse to the side of the keyboard that would best satisfy a "southpaw."

Follow all the steps above to create a model of a computer. Attach the keyboard to the lower edge of the monitor. If you wish, you may construct a special base for the monitor so that the monitor sits vertically like a real computer screen.

Directions for the Teacher

Flag II GLYPH

Focus Skill: The focus skill of this glyph is **math**.

Insight Gained: Students will need to perform **calculations** and **measure**. They will also use **science vocabulary** and look up famous people in **history** and in **visual arts**.

Research Materials:
- Dictionary
- Encyclopedias (print and/or electronic)
- The Internet
- Non-fiction books on painters/famous paintings
- Ruler

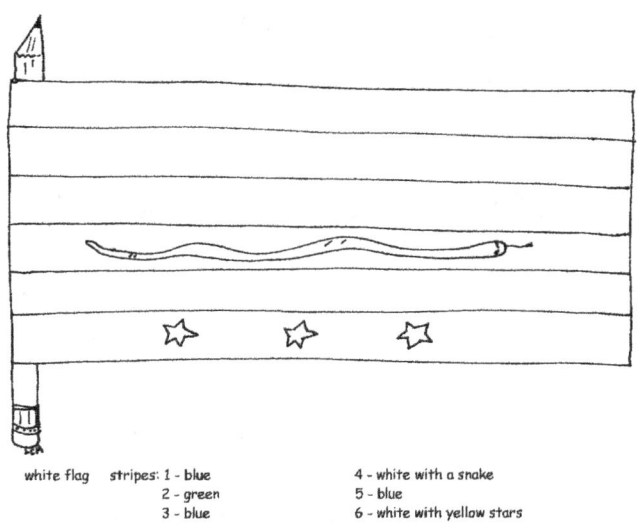

white flag   stripes: 1 - blue   4 - white with a snake
             2 - green   5 - blue
             3 - blue   6 - white with yellow stars

Answer Key:

Students should have a paper flag.

1. The flag is white. There are 220 yards in a furlong. Two hundred twenty mm is equal to 22 cm. The length of the flag is 22 cm; the height is half of that, 11 cm.

2. Starting at the top edge, students should attach or paint stripes. The stripes should be 2 cm tall. The stripes should be blue, since Thomas Gainsborough's famous painting shows a boy dressed in blue.

3. The first white stripe should be colored green, the color of chlorophyll.

4. The next white stripe should have a snake on it.

5. Answers will vary. Students should have yellow stars in the last white stripe. The number of stars should be equal to the number of states the child(ren) have lived in and visited.

6. Since Marie Antoinette said, "Let them eat cake," the flag should have a pole that sticks up 1" past the top edge of the flag. It can be made from a stick, from soda straws, or from pencils attached to the flag.

There should be a total of 6 stripes. The colored blue stripes should be evenly spaced so that white background shows through between each one. Starting at the top edge- the flag stripes are blue, green, blue, white, blue and white.

© Pieces of Learning

Flag II GLYPH

Follow the directions below to create an original flag. Use several different resources for your research. Take careful notes. Be sure to read through all the clues before you begin. Have fun!

___ 1. Cut white paper for the flag. Make its length in mm equal to the number of yards in a furlong. Make the height equal to half the length.

___ 2. Starting at the top edge, put three evenly spaced horizontal stripes on the flag. Make each stripe 2 cm thick. Make the stripes the same color as the clothes the boy is wearing in the famous painting of a child by Thomas Gainsborough.

___ 3. Color the first white stripe the color of chlorophyll.

___ 4. Skip the next colored stripe. On the next white stripe, put the animal that is usually seen on flags along with the phrase "Don't Tread on Me."

___ 5. Put yellow stars on the last white stripe. Make the number of stars equal to the number of U.S. states you (and your partners) have visited. (This includes all the states you've lived in, too!)

___ 6. Who said, "Let them eat cake." If Marie Curie said it, make golden fringe out of yarn and attach it to the bottom edge of the flag. Cut the fringe to be 2" long. If Marie Antoinette said it, make a pole for your flag out of a stick, soda straws or pencils. Have the top of the pole go 1" past the flag's top edge.

Construct your new flag. Re-read the clues and be sure you include all necessary elements. (The flag should have a total of 6 stripes.) Double-check your calculations to be sure the dimensions are accurate.

© Pieces of Learning

Sample Flag II Glyph

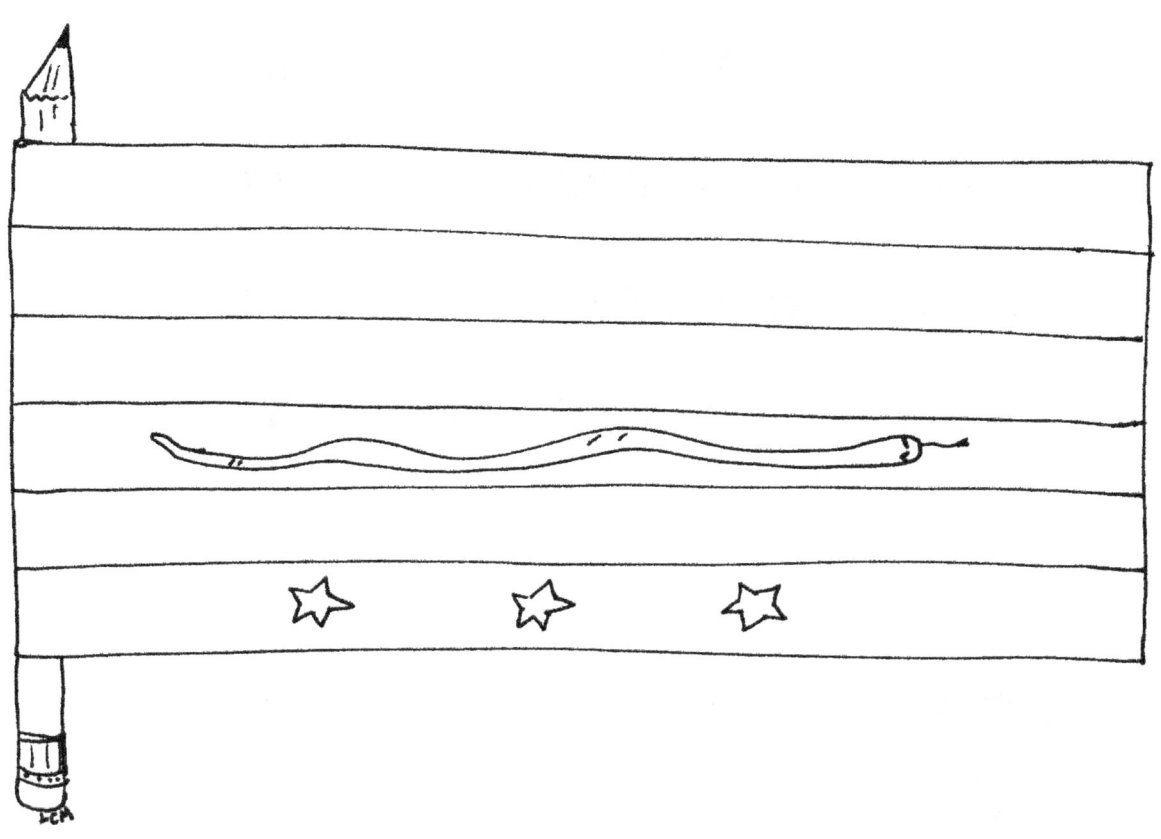

white flag   stripes: 1 - blue   4 - white with a snake
                             2 - green   5 - blue
                             3 - blue   6 - white with yellow stars

Science
GLYPHS

- Collage GLYPH   p. 45
- Fishy Friends GLYPH   p. 47
- Porch Pet GLYPH   p. 49
- Sunshowy Flower GLYPH   p. 51

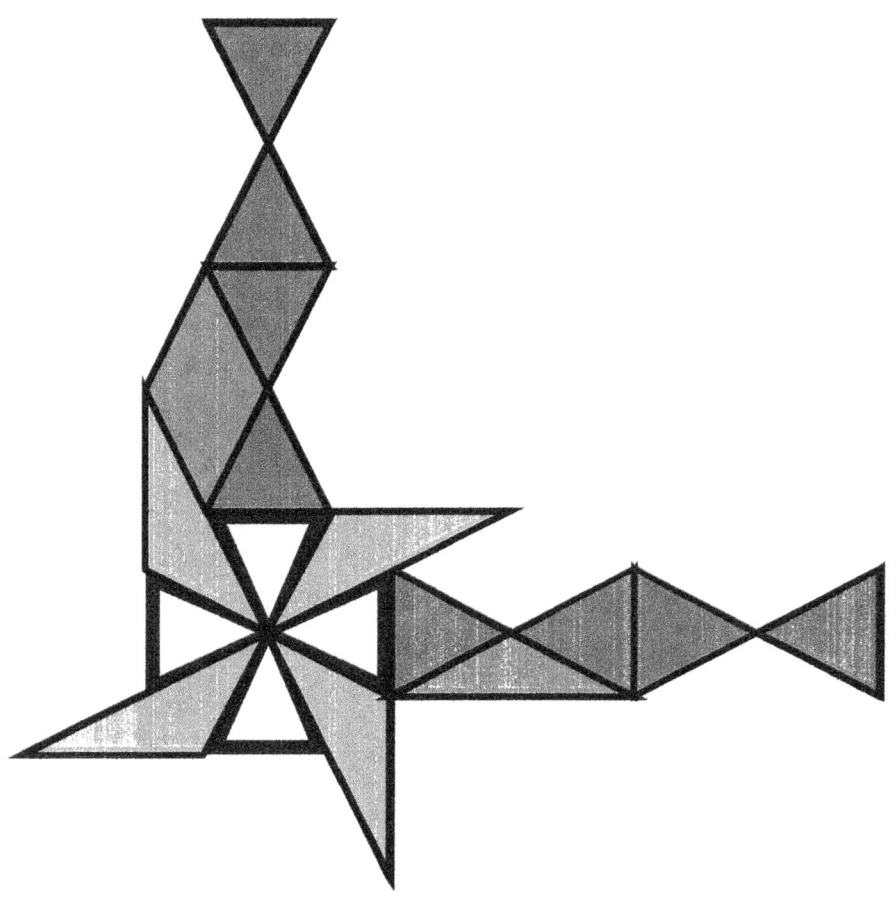

Directions for the Teacher

Collage GLYPH

Focus Skill: The focus skill of this glyph is **science**.

Insight Gained: Students will need to explore the use of **acronyms** and **mnemonic devices** to remember the order of things in **science, math, social studies** and **the arts**.

Research Materials:
- Almanac
- Dictionary
- Encyclopedias (print and/or electronic)
- The Internet
- Non-fiction texts about the solar system, Michigan (the Great Lakes) music theory
- Secondary level science textbook

Answer Key:

The collage may be shown on a poster or large display board. Some acronyms and mnemonic devices have multiple phrases associated with them, so allow for regional/personal differences.

1. The order of the planets is M,V,E,M,J,S,U,N,P, which may stand for **M**y **v**ery **e**xcellent **m**other **j**ust **s**erved **u**s **n**ine **p**izzas. (The collage should show a mother serving pizza, *not* any planets.)

2. The Great Lakes are h, o, m, e, s- **H**uron, **O**ntario, **M**ichigan, **E**rie, **S**uperior

3. The classification of living organisms is k,p,c,o,f,g,s- **K**ing **P**hilip **c**ould **o**nly **f**ind **g**reen **s**ocks (or) **K**ing **P**hyl **c**ame **o**ver **f**or **g**ood **s**paghetti.

4. The notes in the spaces are f, a, c, e (**face**) and the notes on the lines are e, g, b, d, f – **e**very **g**ood **b**oy **d**eserves **f**udge, (or) **d**oes **f**ine.

5. The colors of the rainbow are red, orange, yellow, green, blue, indigo, violet- **Roy G. Biv.**

6. To solve long division, d, m, s, b – **d**irty **M**artin **s**mells **b**ad (or) **D**oes **M**cDonald's® **s**ell **b**urgers? (or) **d**ivide, **m**ultiply, **s**ubtract, **b**ring down (or) **D**ad, **M**om, **S**ister, **B**rother

© Pieces of Learning

Collage GLYPH

Make a collage. Find out what words are said to help remember these well-known acronyms and mnemonic devices. Include images of the <u>helpful phrase</u> in your collage. Remember not to include the actual *subject* that the acronym helps someone remember, just the catchy *phrase*. You may find and use pictures from periodicals, draw original images or use photographs.

*On the back of the collage, write the meaning of each letter of the acronym.

___ 1. M, V, E, M, J, S, U, N, P- the order of planets in our solar system. (Remember, do not picture planets in your collage, but include pictures of what phrase is said to help you remember these letters in order.)

___ 2. H- O- M- E- S- the Great Lakes.

___ 3. K, P, C, O, F, G, S- The classification (taxonomy) of Living Organisms.

___ 4. E, G, B, D, F *and* F, A, C, E- Order of music notes on a staff.

___ 5. Roy G. Biv - The colors of the rainbow.

___ 6. D, M, S, B - The order of steps to solve a long division problem.

Directions for the Teacher

Fishy Friends GLYPH

Focus Skill: The focus skill of this glyph is **science**.

Insight Gained: Students will need to explore several aspects in science as well as use their **measurement skills** and knowledge of **United States history.**

Research Materials:
- Almanac
- Dictionary
- Encyclopedias (print and/or electronic)
- The Internet
- Latin dictionary
- Non-fiction texts about tropical fish
- Ruler

Answer Key:

The fishy friends may be shown on a poster, as puppets or models in front of an appropriate background.

1. A carbon dioxide molecule has two Oxygen atoms. Therefore, there are two fishy friends.

2. Baby blue tang fish are yellow.

3. Carpe diem (4 syllables) means *seize the day* (3 syllables). The fish should have dark blue stripes.

4. Blue tang and the fishy friends live in a coral reef so the drawings or models of the fish should be 6" tall.

5. Students should make a background representing a coral reef that is a 12" x 12" square.

6. Check to see that one fish is glued in the center of the background. The second fish should be in the NW corner of the background at a 45° angle from the center fish.

7. Each fish should be correctly named and labeled. The center fish is named John, since John Wilkes Booth was responsible for Abraham Lincoln's death. The second fish is named Thomas after the inventor of the incandescent light bulb. (Edison.)

© Pieces of Learning

Fishy Friends GLYPH

Follow the directions to create a model or poster of some fishy friends. Use print and on-line sources for your research. Take notes. Be sure to read through all the clues before you begin. Good luck!

____ 1. You will be making some fish. Make the same number of fish as the number of Oxygen atoms in a molecule of Carbon Dioxide.

____ 2. Make fish that are the same color and shape as baby blue tang.

____ 3. Find out what *carpe diem* means in English. Give the fish black stripes if the English translation has the same number of syllables as the Latin term. Give the fish dark blue stripes if it does not.

____ 4. Choosing the appropriate background for the fish will let you know how tall to make your models. (Your fish live along side blue tang.)

      Lagoon – 8"   coral reef – 6"   fresh water pond – 4"

____ 5. Make a picture of the background you chose. Make it 12" x 12".

____ 6. Glue one fish in the center of the background. Glue the other fish in the NW corner of the background at a 45° angle from the center fish.

____ 7. Label each fish with its name. The center fish has the same first name as the man who shot Abraham Lincoln. The second fish shares his name with the inventor of the incandescent light bulb.

Construct the fish. Re-read the clues and be sure your fish are the fishy friends described above.

Directions for the Teacher

Porch Pet GLYPH

Focus Skill: The focus skill of this glyph is **science**.

Insight Gained: Students will need to explore science as well as learn some new **English** and **Spanish vocabulary**. They will also get to experiment with their names or group member names to create a new name.

Research Materials:
- Dictionary
- Encyclopedias (print and/or electronic)
- The Internet
- Non-fiction texts about spiders/arachnids
- Ruler
- Spanish to English dictionary

Answer Key:

Students may complete a drawing or a model of the Porch Pet.

1. Wayne found a spider. The Porch Pet should have two body segments and eight legs.

2. In Spanish, azure is blue and rojo is red. The spider's body should be blue and have red legs.

3. Spiders are found on every continent except Antarctica. The spider should be 6" tall to correspond with the six continents where spiders live.

4. The appropriate background is a web.

5. If something is *variegated* it is varied or different. The Porch Pet's legs should be different somehow, perhaps spotted, striped, etc. They may be different from the body, or may also all be different from each other.

6. Answers will vary. Check to see that the student(s) used letters from his/her name(s) to create a new name.

© Pieces of Learning

Porch Pet GLYPH

Follow the directions to create a rendering of the porch pet. Use print and on-line sources for your research. Take notes. Be sure to read through all the clues before you begin. Good luck!

___ 1. Wayne found a creature on his porch. His brother told him that it was not an insect, but an arachnid. Make the number of body segments and legs accordingly.

___ 2. The creature's body color is what Spanish speakers would call azure. Its legs are rojo.

___ 3. If arachnids are found on 7 continents, make the porch pet 7" tall, if found on only 6 continents, make it 6", etc.

___ 4. Place the arachnid on an appropriate background. It was found on a porch. Would it have come out of a nest, a hole, a web, or a flower's center?

___ 5. The creature's legs are variegated.

___ 6. Give the porch pet a name. Take the letters of your name and rearrange them to create an original name. Write this name on the model of the pet. (If you are working in a group, take the first letters of each group member's first and last names and rearrange them into your original name.)

Show the porch pet that Wayne found. Make a drawing or construct a model using clay, paper, cardboard, or a mixture of several materials. Reread the clues to be sure that you have met all criteria.

Directions for the Teacher

Sunshowy GLYPH

Focus Skill: The focus skill of this glyph is **science**.

Insight Gained: Students will use knowledge in the area of **agriculture/gardening** and strengthen **vocabulary**.

Research Materials:
- Almanac
- Dictionary
- Encyclopedias (print and/or electronic)
- The Internet
- Non-fiction texts about the plants

Answer Key:

The student(s) should prepare a model of the flower. Materials are not specified.

1. The flower itself should be 12" tall.

2. Answers will vary depending upon the state in which you live. However, the Sunshowy should have either two, three or four stems.

3. Tertiary has four syllables, therefore the flower stems should have four petals each. Accept any color that is tertiary, such as blue-green, yellow-orange, etc. Students may show a different tertiary color on each stem- which may be accepted as well.

4. The flower should be shown in sandy soil, made with tan colored clay, paper or paint, since sandy soil drains the best.

5. The Sunshowy would grow well close to the equator. Look for three or more edited sentences with explanations as to why the flower would thrive there. For example, "Regions near the equator are closer to the sun and have warmer weather." Reasons should be written on leaves and attached to the stems of the flowers.

The SUNSHOWY Flower GLYPH

Follow the directions to create a model of the Sunshowy flower. Use print and on-line sources for your research. Take notes. Be sure to read through all the clues before you begin. Good luck!

___ 1. This flower is a perennial. If it blooms only once per season, make it 6" tall. If it blooms every season, make it 12" tall.

___ 2. The Sunshowy flower prefers full sun. Find out which summer month would provide the most sun for where you live. Make the Sunshowy stems accordingly.

    June- 2 stems,   July- 3 stems,   August- 4 stems

___ 3. The blooms on the Sunshowy are a color classified as *tertiary*. You may choose any tertiary color for the blooms on your model. Make the number of petals equal to the number of syllables in the word tertiary.

___ 4. The Sunshowy also likes well-drained soil. Show your model of the flower in the ground in which it would grow best. Show the flower in grassy earth for silt, dark red earth for clay, and tan colored earth for sand.

___ 5. Knowing that the Sunshowy grows best in full sun and well-drained soil, would it grow well close to the equator? Give three reasons why, or why it would not grow well nearest the equator. Write each reason on a leaf and attach the leaves to the flower model stems.

Construct the Sunshowy flower. Re-read the clues and be sure your flower is the true Sunshowy flower.

Social Studies
GLYPHS

➢ The Monster of Nice GLYPH   p. 54

➢ Back to School GLYPH   p. 57

➢ Fan Mail GLYPH   p. 59

➢ Mama's New Hat GLYPH   p. 61

➢ Lighthouse Island GLYPH   p. 63

➢ Make a Map GLYPH   p. 66

➢ Teddy Bear GLYPH   p. 69

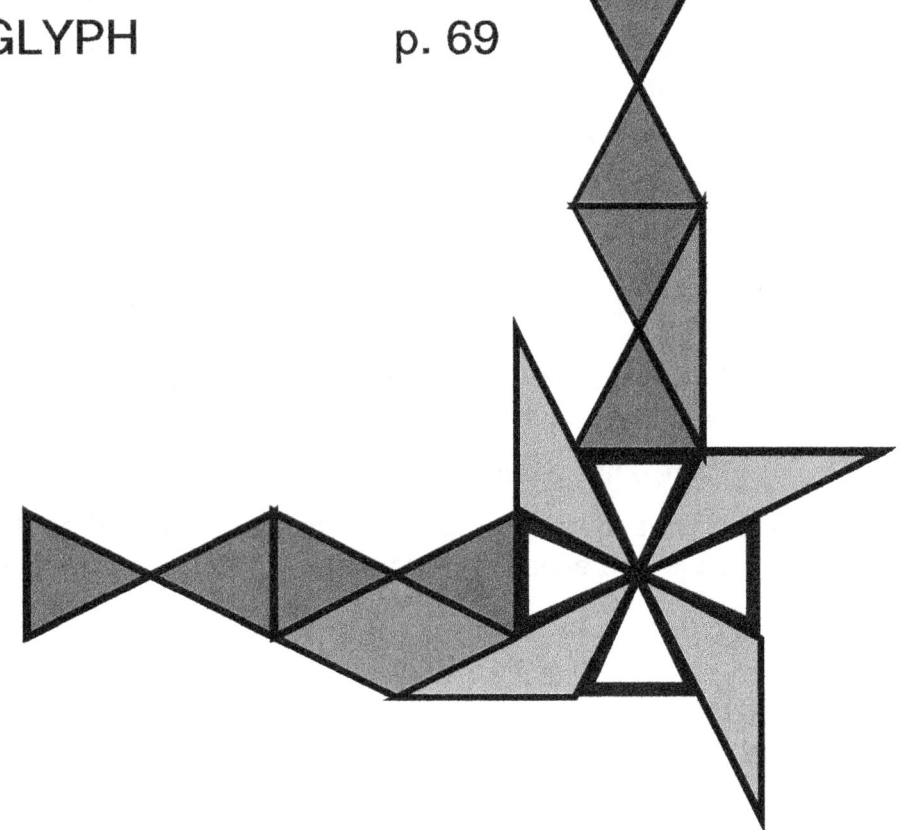

© Pieces of Learning

Directions for the Teacher

The Monster of Nice

Focus Skill: The focus skill of this glyph is **social studies/geography**.

Insight Gained: Students will become more familiar with the geography, language and government of **France**. They will gain practice using an atlas to locate specific geographical locations. They will use a key to figure **distance** on a map.

Research Materials:
- Almanac
- Atlas
- Encyclopedias (print and/or electronic)
- The Internet
- Non-fiction texts about France (provided only after students discover Nice is a city in France)
- Ruler

Answer Key:

1. France is in the Old World- the monster should be 12" tall
2. To reach France from the U.S., one would take a boat or ship- the monster should be fat.
3. Nice is a coastal town- the monster should have a blue body.
4. French and English share the same alphabet- the monster should have pointed teeth. The number is not specified and left up to the student.
5. The population of Nice is >50,000 (@350,000)- the monster should have purple spots.
6. Europe starts with a vowel so the monster should have two feet with five toes on each foot.
7. France has a democratic society so the monster should carry a red flag.
8. Nice is more than 100 miles from Paris and the Eiffel Tower- the monster should have two eyes. The color of the eyes is not specified.

The Monster of Nice GLYPH

Follow the directions to create a model of the monster. Use print and on-line sources for your research. Take notes. Be sure to read through all the clues before you begin. Good luck!

___ 1. If the city of Nice is in the Old World– make your monster 12" tall. If it is in the New World– make the monster 6" tall.

___ 2. If you could drive a car from your house to visit the monster– make him thin. If you would have to take a ship or plane to visit– make him fat.

___ 3. If the monster of Nice lives near the water– make the body blue. If it lives inland– make the body green.

___ 4. If the language spoken in Nice uses the same alphabet letters as English – make the monster have pointed teeth. If the language uses an alphabet different than English– make the teeth rounded.

___ 5. If the population of Nice is below 50,000– make the monster have yellow spots. If the population is greater than 50,000– make the monster have purple spots.

___ 6. If the monster lives on a continent that starts with a consonant– make him have 3 toes on each of his two feet. If he lives on a continent whose name starts with a vowel– make him have 5 toes on his two feet.

___ 7. If the country the monster lives in has a democratic society – make the monster have a red flag in his hand. If the government is not a democracy – make the monster carry a black flag.

___ 8. If the monster is 100 miles or less from the Eiffel Tower – give him one eye. If he is more than 100 miles from that landmark– give him two eyes.

Construct the monster. Re-read the clues and make sure your monster is the true *Monster of Nice*! You may add any missing facial details to the finished monster.

The Monster of Nice GLYPH

blue body

purple spots

red flag

Directions for the Teacher

Back to School GLYPH

Focus Skill: The focus skills of this glyph are **U.S. history** and **geographical terminology.**

Insight Gained: The skills in this glyph are very mixed. Students will become more familiar with the geographical term latitude. They will also need to research **U.S. history** and **policy, art, medicine** and **the stock market**.

Research Materials:
- Atlas
- Dictionary
- Encyclopedias (print and/or electronic)
- Globe
- The Internet
- Newspaper
- Non-fiction texts about art techniques

Answer Key:

1. Yellow is the color used to describe fearful people. A statue of head and shoulders is a bust. Bust-t = bus. They are making a yellow bus.

2. Melbourne's latitude is 37° (50'). The bus should be 37 cm long.

3. The minimum age for becoming U.S. president is 35. There should be five 2 cm square windows because 35÷7=5.

4. The bus should have black and white wheels. Size is not specified.

5. The NYSE has between 7-10 companies under Q. The number of apples on the tree may vary depending upon current newspaper listings. Students determine apple color.

6. Cardiologists specialize in the heart so there should be 3 student silhouettes in bus windows.

7. The symbol for *infinity* (∞) should appear on the hood of the bus.

© Pieces of Learning

Back to School GLYPH

Follow the directions to create a drawing of a common school symbol. Use print and on-line sources for your research. Take notes. Be sure to read through all the clues before you begin. Good luck!

___ 1. First, choose paper that is the color sometimes used to describe someone that is afraid. Then find out what a statue is called when it is only of a person's head and shoulders. Subtract a 't' from this name. What are you making?

___ 2. Look up the latitude of Melbourne. Use this number in centimeters for the length of your picture.

___ 3. Make windows. They should each be 2 cm squared. Take the minimum age for becoming president of the United States and divide it by 7. This total should equal the number of windows you make.

___ 4. Put wheels with hubcaps on your project. Color them using a technique artists would refer to as positive/negative.

___ 5. Craft a tree to stand near the symbol you are making. Add apples to the tree. The number of apples should be equal to the number of publicly traded companies on the New York Stock Exchange under the letter Q.

___ 6. Add some student silhouettes in some of the windows. To determine how many- answer the following question. In what organ does a cardiologist specialize?
    1– brain   2 – lungs   3 – heart   4 – kidneys

___ 7. Make and affix a hood ornament. Use the symbol for *infinity*.

Some elements for the school symbol (like the color of the apples) are not specified. You decide what they should be. Be creative and add details to the drawing.

Directions for the Teacher

Fan Mail GLYPH

Focus Skill: The focus skill of this glyph is **social studies**.

Insight Gained: In addition to looking up pieces of 20th century **American history**, students will practice correctly **addressing a letter**.

Research Materials:
- Almanac
- Calendar
- Dictionary
- Encyclopedias (print and/or electronic)
- Human Resources
- The Internet
- Non-fiction texts about American inventions, famous Black Americans

Answer Key:

The students' answers appear on the front and back of a business envelope, with the exception of the responses to #6, which should be on notebook paper and placed inside the envelope.

1. Joseph Farwell Glidden of Charlestown, New Hampshire, U.S.A. invented barbed wire. An exact street address may not be found, so accept the inventor's name, the town and state.

2. Answers will vary. Check for placement on the envelope, correct two letter USPS state code, and correct capital letters and punctuation.

3. The first African American depicted on a U.S. postage stamp was Booker T. Washington, in 1940. The stamp showed an image of his face.

4. The postmark should have representative wavy cancellation lines and the year should be 1999. Barbed wire was invented in 1874+125 years=1999.

5. The first President's Day of the 21st century was February 21, 2000.

6. (Written on notebook paper and found inside the envelope)

    .com – commerce, .gov – government, .edu – education, .net – network, and .org – organization

7. Regular mail is 1st class mail, therefore the drawn seal on the back of the envelope should be red.

© **Pieces of Learning**

Fan Mail GLYPH

Follow the directions to create a piece of mail. Get a standard business envelope. Follow the directions to prepare your letter. Research the following information using print and on-line sources.

___ 1. Address your letter to the American inventor of barbed wire. Place the information in the proper place on the envelope and be sure to capitalize correctly. Include at least the inventor's city and state. You can make up your own street address.

___ 2. Write your name and your school's address as the return address on the envelope. Use the correct two letter state code for your state as specified by the United States Postal Service.

___ 3. Make a stamp for the NE corner of the envelope. Color it to look like the first postage stamp issued about an African American.

___ 4. Draw a postmark over the stamp. Show the year of the postmark as 125 years after barbed wire was invented.

___ 5. For the month and day of the postmark, use the same month and day as the first President's Day of the 21st century.

___ 6. Look up the following abbreviations found in Internet addresses. Write down what they mean on a piece of notebook paper, fold it in thirds and place it inside the envelope. (Do not seal the envelope.)
– .com   – .net   – .edu   – .gov   – .org

___ 7. Draw a facsimile of a wax seal on the back of the envelope. (Do not seal the envelope.) What class is a regular letter considered? Choose the seal color from the correct answer.

1st class mail- red   2nd class mail- blue   3rd class mail- yellow

Re-read the clues and check your project to be sure your envelope is ready for delivery.

Directions for the Teacher

Mama's New Hat GLYPH

Focus Skill: The focus skill of this glyph is **social studies.**

Insight Gained: In addition to looking up **history** and **geography items**, students will need to explore several 'common knowledge' aspects.

Research Materials:
- Almanac
- Calendar
- Dictionary
- Encyclopedias (print and/or electronic)
- Human Resources
- The Internet
- Non-fiction texts about dogs

Answer Key:

The students should complete a drawing of Mama's New Hat. Size of finished drawing is not specified. It is acceptable for students to have added additional details not listed below, permitting that they do not interfere with the assessment of the required elements.

1. It was straw that broke the camel's back. Mama's hat is straw.

2. One of the Seven Wonders of the World was the Hanging Gardens of Babylon.

3. Knowing the above, students should include either six or eight flowers or other pieces of foliage.

4. The Jamaican flag is green, black and yellow. The flowers adorning the hat should be green, black and yellow.

5. A Chow Chow's tongue is blue. Mama's hat should have a blue ribbon

   tied in a square knot.

6. The drawing should be labeled 'Memorial Day.'

© Pieces of Learning

Mama's New Hat GLYPH

Follow the directions to create a drawing of a new hat. Use print and on-line sources for your research. Take notes. Be sure to read through all the clues before you begin. Good luck!

___ 1. Mama has a new hat. It is made out of the same material that "broke the camel's back." Depict this material in your drawing.

___ 2. The hat has items glued to the brim. Some of these items are like those that would have been found in Babylon at one of the seven wonders of the world.

___ 3. Make such representative items and affix them to your hat picture. Make an even number of them that is greater than 5 but less than 10.

___ 4. Make them in the same colors as the colors in the Jamaican flag.

___ 5. Add a ribbon to the hat that is the color of a Chow Chow's tongue. Show the ribbon tied in a square knot.

___ 6. Mama will wear her hat on a holiday in May that celebrates the United States' armed forces. Label the picture with the name of this holiday.

Make a drawing of Mama's new hat. Re-read the clues and make sure that you add all the details described above. You may add a few additional details of your own.

Directions for the Teacher

Lighthouse Island GLYPH

Focus Skill: The focus skill of this glyph is **geography**.

Insight Gained: Students will find a lighthouse in the U.S. as well as use **longitude** and **latitude** to find out what lands are near this newly discovered island. They will also use **math skills** and research **American history.**

Research Materials:
- Atlas
- Encyclopedias (print and/or electronic)
- The Internet
- Non-fiction texts about lighthouses, Alaska, and American history
- Ruler

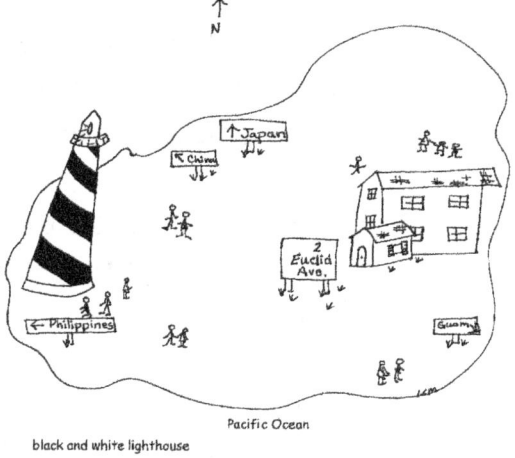

black and white lighthouse

Answer Key:
Students should complete a model of the island. Ideally it will have additions that are three dimensional.

1. Twelve pennies side to side are approximately 23 cm long, therefore the diameter of the island is 23 cm.
2. The lighthouse on the western side should look like the lighthouse on Cape Hatteras, which has a black and white "candy cane" design.
3. A latitude of 20° and a longitude of 140° is in the Pacific Ocean, south of the Tropic of Cancer. On the island students should label nearby countries with directional arrows. For example: The Philippines is W, Japan is N, China is NW, and Guam is SE of the island.
4. The length of the cottage is 12 cm, 2/3 of 12 is 8, so the height of the cottage is 8 cm. Color is not specified.
5. The address marker may be on the cottage or on a post near the cottage. The United States paid $0.02 an acre for the land in Alaska, so the street number is two.
6. Euclid is considered the father of geometry, so the address marker should read 2 Euclid. Students may add *Street, Road, Avenue*, etc. to the name.
7. There were thirteen original colonies, so there should be 13 visitors on the island.

Many details such as the size of the lighthouse or visitors is unspecified so the students have some decision making. They should be creative and add foliage and wildlife to the island.

© Pieces of Learning

Lighthouse Island GLYPH

Follow the directions to create a model of a newly discovered island. Use paper, cardboard, and any other materials you think will create a creative, attractive model. Follow the steps below to complete it.

___ 1. Place twelve pennies end to end in a straight line (a flat line, not a stack.) Measure them in cm. Make the diameter of your island model equal to this number.

___ 2. Place a lighthouse on the western coast of the island. Draw the design on the lighthouse exactly like that of the lighthouse on Cape Hatteras.

___ 3. Your island is at a latitude of 20° and a longitude of 140°, just south of the Tropic of Cancer. What countries are near this island? Label them on your island with directional arrows. Write the direction on the arrow. (For example: The United States is Northeast of Hawaii, so on a map of Hawaii, you would put ↗ to U.S. A.)

___ 4. Make a small model cottage for your island. The length of the cottage should be 12 cm. Make it so that its height is 2/3 of the length.

___ 5. Make an address marker for the cottage. The street number will be the same number as the amount of money per acre that the United States paid when it bought land in what is now the state of Alaska.

___ 6. The street name will be named for the famous Greek mathematician who is considered the father of geometry.

___ 7. Put some visitors on the island. Make the number of visitors equal to the number of original colonies in the United States.

Collect all information necessary to make an accurate model of the new island. Be creative. Add details to your island such as plants and wildlife.

Sample Lighthouse Island Glyph

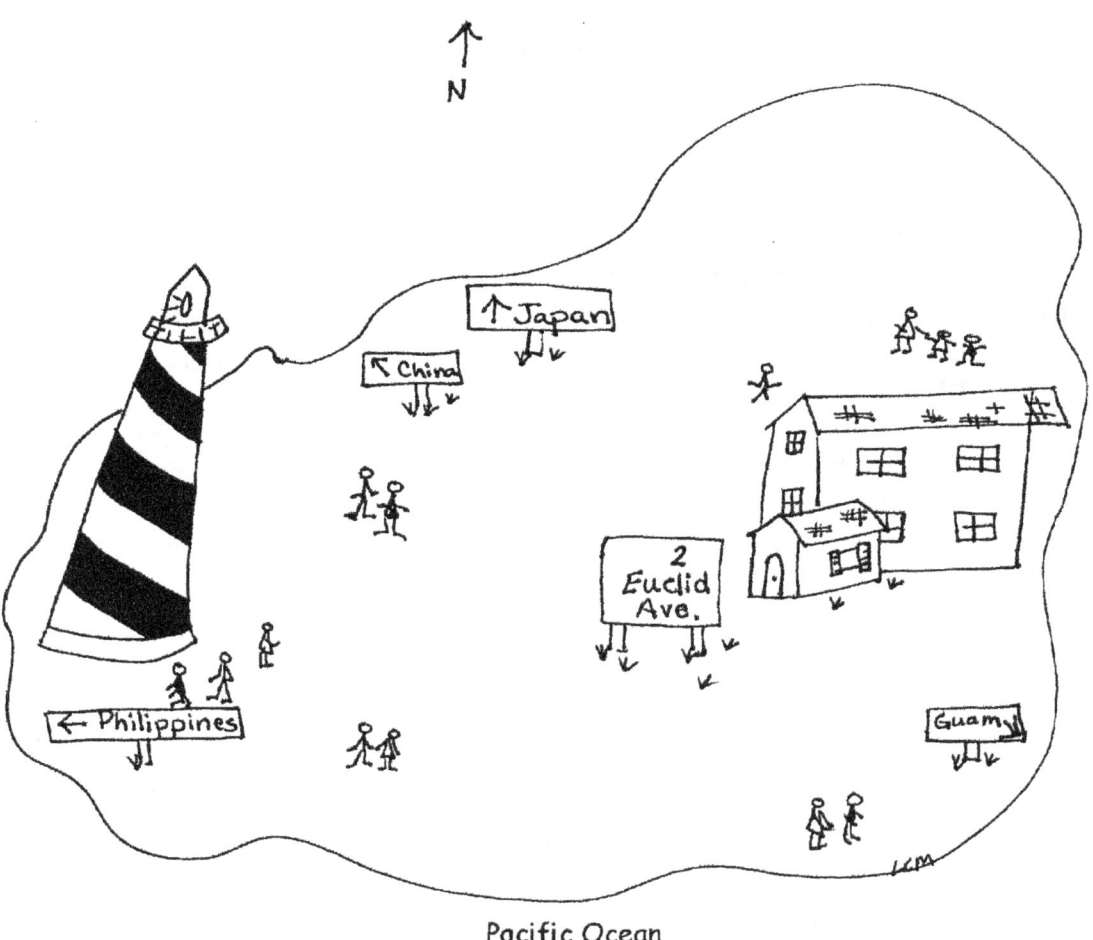

Pacific Ocean

black and white lighthouse

Directions for the Teacher

Make a Map GLYPH

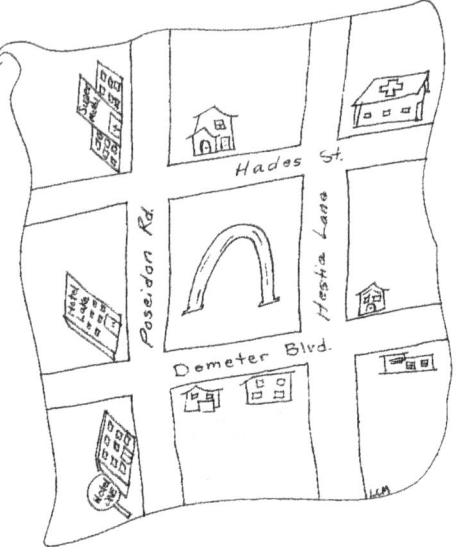

Focus Skill: The focus skill of this glyph is **social studies**.

Insight Gained: In addition to researching a **famous American** person and city, students will be challenged to find out about a famous American writer. They will use their **math, mapping**, and **artistic skills** to complete a **map**.

Research Materials:
- Dictionary
- Encyclopedias (print and/or electronic)
- Literary works by Faulkner
- The Internet
- Non-fiction text about Greek mythology
- Ruler
- Rules for the game Monopoly, or human resources

Answer Key:

Students should complete a map on 12" x 18" light colored paper. Details added to the map may be flat or relief. Students were asked to be creative and add foliage and/or animals to the map.

1. The map should show the name *Yoknapatawpha,* the fictitious county referred to in Faulkner stories.
2. The map will have 4 streets, laid out by two sets of parallel lines perpendicular to each other. (Two streets run east/west, two run north/south.)
3. Clara Barton started the American Red Cross. The red cross medical symbol is appropriate and should be on a building (of any shape and color) in the northeast part of town.
4. St. Louis, Missouri is famous for their arch. A similar landmark should be in the center of the map.
5. Having four houses on the same property in Monopoly allows you to buy a hotel. There should be three hotels on one of the vertically running streets on the map.
6. Streets should have any of the following names of Zeus' brothers and sisters: Poseidon, Hades, Hestia, Demeter, Hera.
7. The map should have 5 houses on horizontal streets. Brown if your school is less than 15 years old, yellow if older than 15 years.

Make a Map GLYPH

Make a map. Start with a 12" x 18" piece of paper. Choose a light, neutral color. Follow the directions below and find the appropriate information so that your map is complete.

___ 1. The name on the map will be the same as a fictional county mentioned in many novels and short stories by W. Faulkner. Find out the name of this county and write in on the northern border of the map. Draw a compass rose below it.

___ 2. Create four main streets for the town. Make your map show two sets of parallel lines. One set should be perpendicular to the other set.

___ 3. Find out what organization Clara Barton started. Use an appropriate symbol and put it on a building that is in the northeast part of town on your map.

___ 4. Put a landmark in the center of town. Find out what unusual piece of architecture is in St. Louis, Missouri and put a similar structure on your map.

___ 5. When you have four houses on the same property in the game Monopoly what can you buy? Put three of them on one vertically running street.

___ 6. Name your streets. Use the names of any of the brothers and sisters of Zeus.

___ 7. If your school is less than 15 years old, add 5 brown houses to the horizontal streets. If your school is greater than 15 years old, add 5 yellow houses to the horizontal streets.

Follow the directions. Check your notes and be sure you have all the correct inclusions for your map. Be creative and colorful when you write names on the map and create buildings. Add some animals and foliage to the map.

© Pieces of Learning

Sample Make A Map Glyph

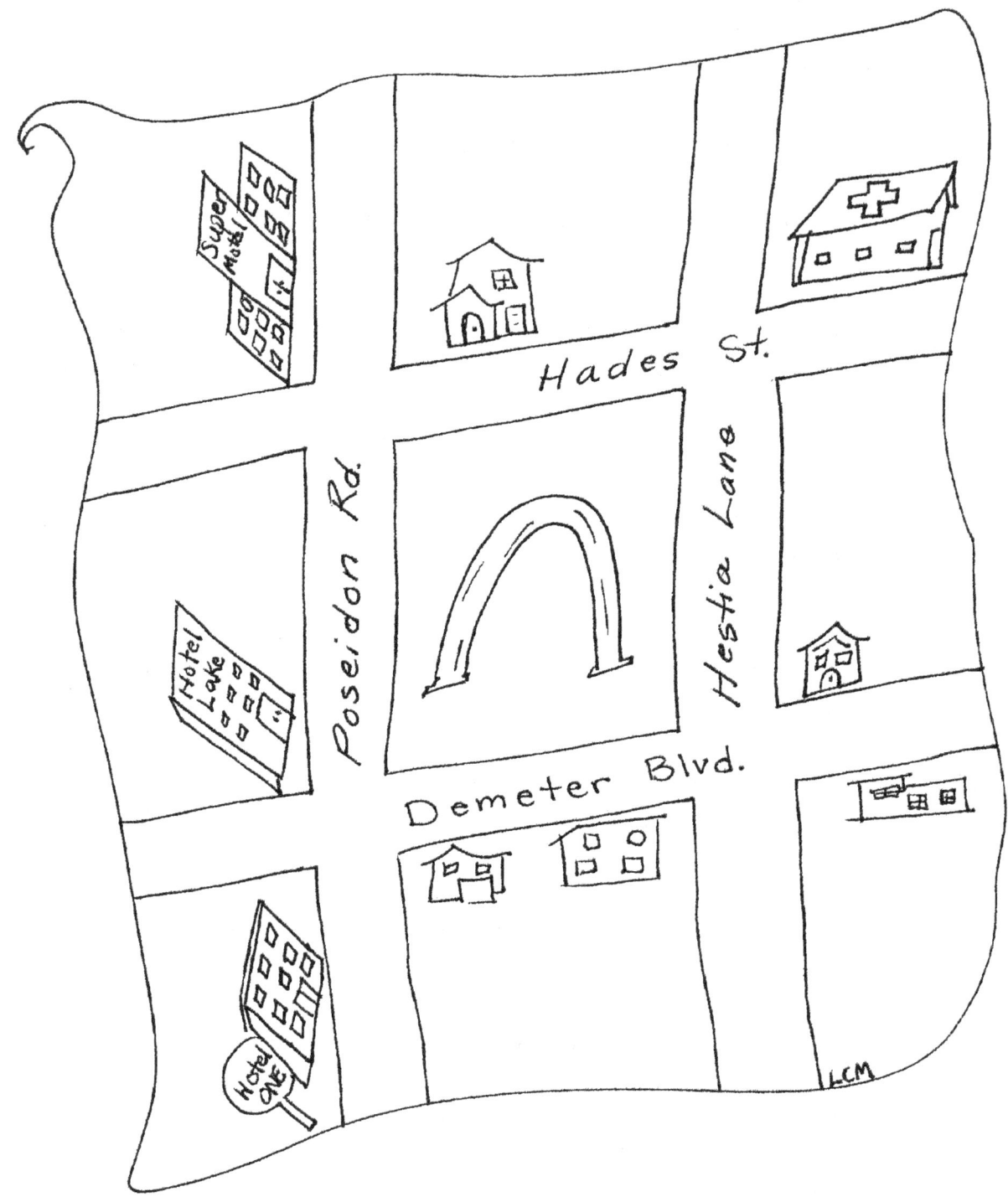

Directions for the Teacher

Teddy Bear GLYPH

Focus Skill: The focus skill of this glyph is **Fine Arts.**

Insight Gained: In addition to some **math**, the students will discover information about **music history, theory, a famous musical,** and **visual art.**

Research Materials:
- Atlas
- The Internet
- Non-fiction books about bears
- Non-fiction books about color and art history
- Non-fiction books about music history and theory

brown bear red hat

Answer Key:

1. When red, yellow and blue are mixed it creates a brown color, so the bear should be brown.

2. The area code in Montana is 406, divided by 10= 40.6. The bear should be 40 cm high.

3. Common time, also known as 4/4 time, has 4 beats per measure. The bear gets 4 buttons, any color or shape is acceptable.

4. In the famous painting, Whistler's mother is sitting in a rocking chair. The bear should be depicted sitting in a rocking chair and facing west.

5. The bear should be wearing a lapel pin with T. Roosevelt written on it since the teddy bear got its name from Theodore Roosevelt.

6. Seventy-six trombones led the big parade. The price tag should read $76.00.

7. A collar with a Baroque composer's name should be around the bear's neck. Some examples of Baroque composers are Handel, J.S. Bach, and Vivaldi.

8. Bears live in every continent but Antarctica. The bear gets a red hat.

Teddy Bear GLYPH

Follow the directions to create a teddy bear. Use paper and paint to show the new friend. Research the following information using print and on-line sources.

___ 1. Choose the paper or paint for your teddy bear. Use the color you get when you mix all three primary colors together.

___ 2. Take the area code of Montana and divide it by 10. Make the bear's height equal to this number in cm.

___ 3. How many beats per measure are there in *common time*? Put this number of buttons on the bear. You decide the color and shape for the buttons.

___ 4. The teddy bear needs a rest. Picture the teddy bear on the same type of furniture that Whistler's Mother is sitting on in the famous painting "Portrait of Artist's Mother."

___ 5. Give the bear a lapel pin. Make the pin show the name of the president of the United States for which the teddy bear received its nickname.

___ 6. Give your bear a price tag. The amount in dollars is equal to the number of trombones in a song sung by the character Harold Hill in the Music Man.

___ 7. Name your bear and place its name on a collar around its neck. Give the bear the name of a Baroque composer.

___ 8. If some species of bear lives on all 7 continents, give the bear a blue hat. If bears inhabit 6 or fewer continents, give the bear a red hat.

Check back over the directions and make sure your bear has all the required attributes. No specifications are given for the bear's general outline or facial features. Use your creativity and add details.

Sample Teddy Bear Glyph

brown bear   red hat

Appendix

- GLYPH Research Checklist — p. 73
- Research Practice- Almanac — p. 74
- Research Practice- Atlas — p. 76
- Research Practice- Encyclopedia — p. 78

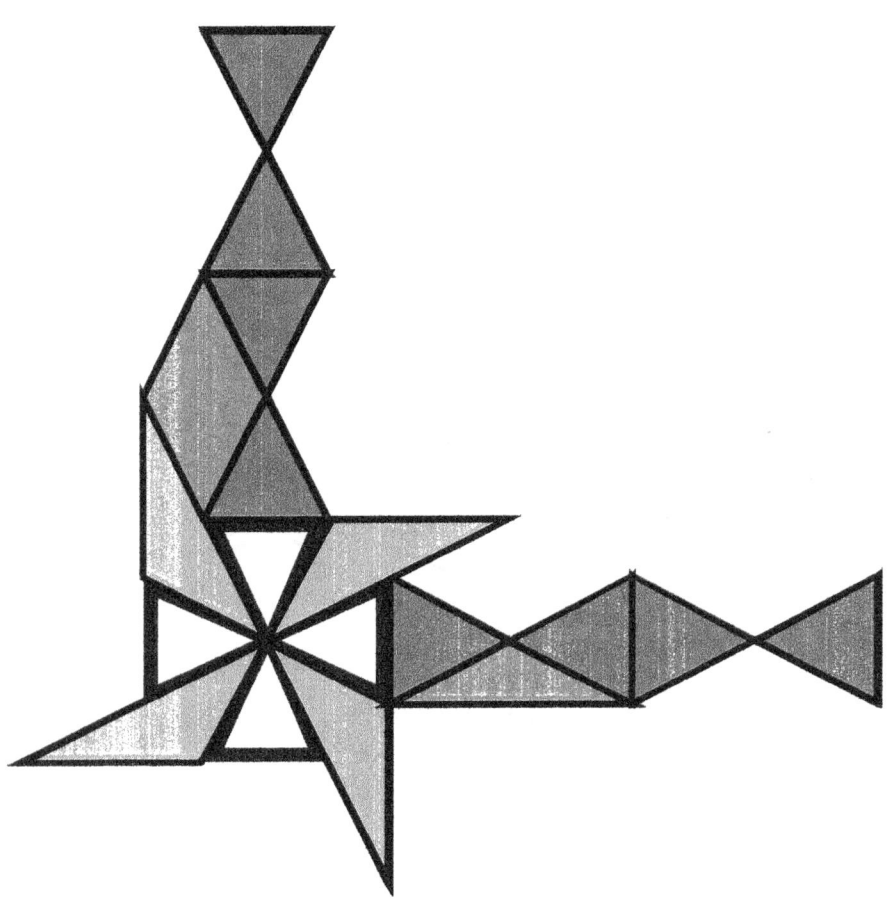

GLYPH Research Checklist

Use this checklist to help guide your research when completing a GLYPH.

RESEARCH TIPS

* Write *neatly.*
* Read carefully.
* Notes do not have to be written in complete sentences.
* Be short and concise.
* Use abbreviations.
* Show your math calculations and double check your work.
* Use multiple resources.
* Get help from the media specialist if you need it.
* **Expect to succeed!**

I am working on the _____ GLYPH

Research Tools to Use:

__ Non-Fiction Books about _____

__ Encyclopedia (print)   __ Encyclopedia (electronic)

__ Atlas   __ Almanac

__ Dictionary   __ Human Resources (ask someone)

__ Internet (search engines, AskJeeves.com, etc.)

__ Newspaper   __ Upper level math or science text

__ Other _____   __ Other _____

© **Pieces of Learning**

Almanac Practice

Name_____Date_____

Almanacs contain a variety of information. Answer the following questions and you will become more familiar with what type of information the almanac has to offer.

1. Almanacs contain many lists, such as a list of all the Presidents of the United States. Find another list in the almanac. Write below the subject of the list you found.

_____

2. Almanacs can tell you the biggest, tallest, shortest, longest of some things. Find an example.

    Biggest _____

    Tallest _____

    Shortest _____

    Longest _____

3. Find the pages in the almanac that show pictures of flags from around the world.
    How many flags have stars? _____
    Stripes?_____

4. An almanac shares information in graphs and charts. Find two different graphs or charts. Write what information each one shares.

Graph #1 _____

Graph #2 _____

5. You can find out a lot about other countries. Look up a country. List its language, population, some native plants and animals, and one fact about its history.

Country _____

Language _____

Population _____

Native Plants _____

Native Animals _____

Historical Fact _____

6. Look in the Table of Contents. On the back of this paper record all the different subject headings about which you can find information in this reference book.

7. Wacky facts are sometimes included in an almanac. Can you find an odd, wacky fact? List it.

_____

Atlas Practice

Name_____ Date_____

An atlas contains many maps. Some may show large areas like whole continents or countries. Some may show specific cities. But an atlas also tells much more. Use an atlas to answer the questions below.
*Remember to capitalize proper nouns.

1. Does your atlas contain a map of the world?   Yes   No
   Does your atlas show individual continents?   Yes   No
   Does it show individual countries?   Yes   No
   Does your atlas show what scientists think the land on earth was like before the continents moved to where they are now?   Yes   No
   If so, what is this land mass called? _____

1. Does the atlas contain maps that show natural resources? If so, list three places that refine oil.

   _____

   _____

   _____

3. List three places that harvest wood or wood products.

   _____

   _____

   _____

4. Find a chart in an atlas that shows time zones across the world. What is the nearest country to the International Date Line?

   _____

76   © **Pieces of Learning**

5. How many hours ahead of Texas is London? _____

6. Find maps showing topography (land features.) Name three places that have very high mountains.

   _____

   _____

   _____

2. Look at a map of the state in which you live. Find out two new facts about your state. Write them here.

   _____

   _____

   _____

   _____

3. Find an atlas that shows the populations of different locations.

   Name a location with a population of over 5,000,000. _____

   Name a location with a population of over 1,000,000. _____

   Name a location with a population of over 500,000. _____

© Pieces of Learning

Encyclopedia Practice

Name _____ Date _____

    Encyclopedias contain articles in alphabetical order. In print encyclopedias, these articles are in several, bound volumes. An on-line/electronic encyclopedia allows you to search for and retrieve the articles you request. This research source can inform you about places in the world, influential and important people, scientific discoveries and principles.

    Remember – when you take notes and then use information you have learned from an encyclopedia, you must restate the information *in your own words*.

    Use appropriate volumes of an encyclopedia to answer the following questions. Answer the questions with complete sentences.

1. Look at the spines of a set of encyclopedias. Why do you think some volumes contain articles that all start with one letter of the alphabet while other volumes contain articles that start with several letters?

_____

_____

2. Look up a famous person about whom you would like to know more. Read the entry article about them. Write two new facts that you have learned about the person.

    1. _____

    2. _____

3. Look up the country of Cameroon. Write two facts that are new to you.

1. _____

2. _____

Many times an article will be cross-referenced. This means that the encyclopedia refers you to another article that has related information. The cross-reference is usually next to the entry or at the end of the article. Look for the words *see also:* when looking for a cross-reference.

4. Look up Alfred Russel Wallace. Write the cross-reference that is suggested.

see also: _____

5. Is there anyone famous with a name like yours? Or maybe a famous place or invention? Look up your last name in an encyclopedia. What entry article is the closest to your name?

_____

Write a brief description.

_____

_____

_____

_____

_____

_____

© **Pieces of Learning**